DECORATING YOUR FIRST APARTMENT

DECORATING YOUR FIRST APARTMENT

from moving in
to making it your own

paige gilchrist

LARK BOOKS

A DIVISION OF STERLING PUBLISHING CO., INC.
NEW YORK, NY

EDITOR:
PAIGE GILCHRIST

ART DIRECTOR:
CHRIS BRYANT

COVER DESIGN:
BARBARA ZARETSKY

PHOTOGRAPHER:
**WRIGHT CREATIVE
PHOTOGRAPHY & DESIGN**

ASSISTANT EDITORS:
**VERONIKA ALICE GUNTER
HEATHER SMITH**

EDITORIAL ASSISTANT:
RAIN NEWCOMB

EDITORIAL INTERNS:
**ANNE WOLFF HOLLYFIELD
NATHALIE MORNU**

ILLUSTRATOR:
BERNADETTE WOLF

PRODUCTION ASSISTANT:
HANNES CHAREN

SPECIAL PHOTOGRAPHY:
SANOMA SYNDICATION

Alexander van Berge

Dennis Brandsma

John Dummer

Hotze Eisma

Rene Gonkel

John van Groenedaal

Paul Grootes

Peter Kooijman

Louis Lemaire

Otto Polman

Dolf Straatemeier

Carel Verduin

Library of Congress Cataloging-in-Publication Data

Gilchrist, Paige.
    Decorating your first apartment : from moving in to making your own /
by Paige Gilchrist.—1st ed.
      p. cm.
    ISBN 1-57990-335-5
    1. Apartments. 2. Interior decoration. I. Title.

  NK2195.A6 G55 2002
  747'.88314—dc21
                                             2002020206

10 9 8 7 6 5 4 3 2 1

First Edition

Published by Lark Books,
a division of Sterling Publishing Co., Inc.
387 Park Avenue South, New York, N.Y. 10016

© 2002, Lark Books

Distributed in Canada by Sterling Publishing,
c/o Canadian Manda Group, One Atlantic Ave., Suite 105
Toronto, Ontario, Canada M6K 3E7

Distributed in the U.K. by Guild of Master Craftsman Publications Ltd.,
Castle Place, 166 High Street, Lewes, East Sussex, England BN7 1XU
Tel: (+ 44) 1273 477374, Fax: (+ 44) 1273 478606
Email: pubs@thegmcgroup.com, Web: www.gmcpublications.com

Distributed in Australia by Capricorn Link (Australia) Pty Ltd.,
P.O. Box 704, Windsor, NSW 2756 Australia

If you have questions or comments about this book, please contact:
Lark Books • 67 Broadway, Asheville, NC 28801 • (828) 253-0467

Manufactured in China

ISBN 1-57990-335-5

contents

introduction

YOUR REFUGE. YOUR SHOWPLACE. YOUR ALTER EGO. Your party palace. Regardless of how you see it, the point is, your first apartment is *yours*. How you transform it into the kind of place you want to live in is totally up to you.

Trouble is, if you give it awhile, that empowering little phrase—*totally up to you*—starts running as a haunting continuous loop inside your head. Pretty soon you're feeling like the main character in a bad sitcom, stuck in an episode that does not end well. You can hear the canned laughter swell and see the credits roll as you picture yourself, chin in hands, sitting on a plastic crate in the middle of a room that features nothing but a tacked-up concert poster and the desk lamp you took to college.

This book is here to help you snap out of it. Our goal is not to pressure you into thinking your apartment must spring to life, intact, from the pages of a trendy interior decorating magazine. It's also not to encourage you to clutter your space with a bunch of junk you don't really care about or need. Instead, we're here to help you realize that you're busy, you're on a budget, you're pretty new to this, and yet it's still possible to create a place that has character and style—not to mention furniture, curtains, and a few accents on the walls.

Decorating your first apartment is essentially about making yourself at home. That means it's a pursuit that's part practical *(How do I hang a shelf?)* and part creative *(Wonder how this chair would look painted chartreuse.)*. We appeal to both sides of your brain with sensible how-to advice, imaginative yet doable projects, and page after page of inspiring, full-color ideas and examples.

the BASICS

The book's opening chapter is one of those mini-handbooks for life you always thought someone should research and write for you. It's divided into six handy sections. The Hunt is for those still in search of the right place. It covers everything from spotting potential problems with apartments to sizing up landlords. The Red Tape walks you through all the paperwork of renting. The Layout shows you how to make yourself a simple floor plan and figure out what goes where, Sprucing Up gives you the handy-person basics of everything from painting walls to refinishing furniture, Settling In is a series of cheat sheets to remind you of all those essentials (corkscrews to bath mats), and Keeping Clean is a section you'll eventually be glad you have as a reference. If you're not in the mood for these nuts and bolts right now, feel free to flip right to the heart of the book.

the DECORATING PROJECTS & IDEAS

Realizing that first apartments, like first kisses and first jobs, are often not perfect, in the book's main chapters we break apartments down into their surface elements: walls, floors, and windows. We show you step-by-step approaches for turning whatever surrounds you, perfect or not, into design features that work *for* you, rather than problems that sabotage your look. Then we move on to chapters full of dozens of inventive ways to use lighting, furniture, accessories, and clever storage tactics to turn your apartment's bare rooms into a place you're proud to call home. Oh, and don't worry. We don't suddenly forget those irritating little details—money and time. You don't need a trust fund and several personal assistants who happen to have attended design school to pull these projects off.

the DISCLAIMER

You also don't need an apartment that looks just like one of the ones we've photographed or the exact same chair, lamp, paint color, or potted plant we've used. Though we give you detailed instructions so you can replicate any project in the book, we also give you plenty of permission—along with hints, tips, idea starters, and loads of helpful sidebars—for adapting everything to suit your own setting and style.

Whether you already have a clear idea what that style is (maybe you're committed to retro kitsch) or you're just starting to experiment (a little Zen minimalism here, a touch of ethnic flair there), *Decorating Your First Apartment* can help you sort out what you want and then pull it all together. Which brings you right back to where you started. How your apartment looks *is* totally up to you—you just don't have to think of everything yourself.

BASICS

Before we launch right into the specifics of stitching beaded fringe onto throw pillows and turning Asian-print fabric into no-sew curtains, we thought we'd offer this handy overview of the basics of apartment dwelling and decorating. How can you worry about fringe and fabric, after all, when you still don't have a clue where you're going to put everything (we show you how to mark out a simple floor plan) or have any idea what tools you need to hang your pictures and put your shelves together (easy; see the chart on page 37). If you're a true plan-ahead type—meaning you picked up this book before you even have an apartment— you're in luck. We also offer tips on finding the right place for you and on muddling through the paperwork it takes to make it yours.

the hunt

Apartments come in the form of spacious lofts carved out of old industrial buildings, homey efficiencies in converted Victorian houses, modern flats in complexes with swimming pools and fitness centers, and plenty of low-ceilinged shoe boxes in run-of-the-mill high-rises. Much of your decision about which apartment is the right one for you will be based on what's available where you need it, when you need it, at a price you can afford. Part of it will also be based on personal priorities; maybe you're willing to sacrifice closet space if the apartment comes with a patio, or you'll settle for a smaller place if it has hardwood floors. Once you've narrowed your options using your individual criteria, here are some more general measures you can use to make your final decision.

FIRST 10 QUESTIONS TO ASK ABOUT ANY APARTMENT

It's easy to come up with a short list of potential apartments simply by working your way down the classifieds over the phone. Here's a list of 10 basic questions that'll help you narrow the possibilities.

1. How much is rent, and when is it due? (Is there a grace period? Is there a penalty for late payment?)

2. How much is the deposit? (Under what conditions is it held?)

3. Is the apartment furnished or unfurnished?

4. Are all the appliances, the plumbing, the heat, and the air conditioning in good working order?

5. Who do I contact for repairs when they're necessary? (Are maintenance hours restricted? How is emergency service handled?)

6. Are utilities furnished? (What about parking, extra storage, or garbage and recycling services?)

7. What can you tell me about the neighbors and the neighborhood?

8. Am I allowed to have pets? (Overnight guests?)

9. Can I sublease or get roommates?

10. When could I move in?

■ Take a pencil and paper with you. We're aware of the fact that if this tip were coming from your mother, you'd roll your eyes. Don't worry; she never needs to know you're following our practical advice for taking stock of your potential new place. As you visit each room of the apartment you're considering, jot down any concerns or questions.

■ Move furniture so you can see every inch of wall, floor, and ceiling. If the linoleum has been peeled up on part of the bathroom floor or there's a gouge in the wall behind the current resident's couch, you want to know it now.

■ Get on your hands and knees or stand on a chair to explore questionable areas, if necessary. Forget whether this makes you feel silly; now is the time to investigate where that strange smell is coming from or how much storage space really exists above the bedroom closet.

■ Stand still and listen. Keep an ear out for problems in the apartment (loud heating or cooling systems, drips) as well as noisy neighbors and traffic. Open and close windows and doors.

■ Test the appliances.

■ Note if the apartment or the building it's housed in feature any of the signs of trouble listed below.

evaluating an apartment

Some landlords disguise problems with their property. Others are honest but oblivious. Sizing up an apartment with a sharp eye before you're locked into a year-long lease can help you avoid—or negotiate solutions to—problems that could cost you money, peace of mind, or your well-being later on.

TELLTALE TROUBLES

1. Exposed wires, faulty electrical appliances, scorch marks, smoke damage

2. Lack of emergency exits or smoke alarms, or blocked exits

3. Pet odors or damage on carpets, floors, or walls

4. Water stains near toilets, tubs, or sinks, or temporary fixes on drains (all suggest faulty plumbing)

5. Discolored floors, ceilings, or windowsills (they probably mean water damage)

6. Holes in the walls

7. Mouse droppings, cockroaches, flies, ants, or other indications of pests

8. Leaky or broken windows, or windows that don't open smoothly

9. Cluttered or damaged entryways, halls, or stairs in a multi-unit building

10. Loud, unruly, or generally unneighborly neighbors

When you're finished looking over the apartment, if you're interested, discuss your list of questions and concerns with the landlord—and don't rent the space until you're satisfied with the explanations and/or improvement plans.

DID YOU KNOW?

Utility companies can tell you how much they charged previous tenants for water, electricity, gas, and oil—just call them.

Have the exact address handy and, if possible, the name of the person who holds the current account. (The name is not always necessary.) When calling, ask how many days are in the billing cycle, and ask for both the highest single cost and average cost based on one year of service. Most utility companies will provide this information over the phone.

landlords:

they come with the lease

In days of yore, landlords didn't just own land—they ruled it. Anyone inhabiting the area was a tenant, subject to the landlord's whims and expected to show unwavering gratitude. (This arrangement still exists today. It's known as living at home.)

Now, customs and laws grant tenants rights when inhabiting a rented home sweet home. But the landlord remains a person you'll interact with throughout the time of your lease, whether your hot water heater is acting up or your upstairs neighbors are. Use the following suggestions to find one you'll like leasing from.

POTENTIAL LANDLORDS AND THEIR POSITIVE SIGNS

THEY'RE FORTHRIGHT AND WELCOMING.

This doesn't mean they must be super friendly or socially skilled. It does mean they provide all relevant details and stipulations for living in the property and respond thoroughly to your questions when you're checking it out (if you need some help figuring out what those questions should be, look back at First 10 Questions, page 11). Their candor and command of the facts at this early stage suggest that there won't be many surprises—such as newly imposed rules — during the term of your lease.

THEY'RE REASONABLE.

They understand that tenants will be living full and varied lives in their apartments. In your case, that could mean pet canaries, daily drum practice, a bike that needs storing—or all of the above. They discuss your specific needs and any concerns you have about the terms of the lease or condition of the apartment. When you explain your needs, they're willing to compromise a bit.

THEY CARE ABOUT THE PROPERTY.

A landlord who, while showing you around, suggests the sunniest spot for your kitchen table or is sincerely enthusiastic about the new paint job in the bathroom is someone who has thought about what it's like to live in the space he's renting. This is good. He wants you to enjoy living there—either because he's proud of the apartment or because his income is based primarily on your rent check, or both. Landlords who see their property as an investment to be cared for tend to work with tenants to avoid problems and alleviate turnover.

THEY'RE COMPATIBLE WITH YOU.

A landlord's style is usually obvious: she's firm or lenient, prompt or leisurely, etc. What's yours? Do you pay your bills like clockwork and expect others to honor their obligations? Choose a like-minded landlord, and she'll likely reward your reliability with good service when it comes to a leaking roof or clogged drain. Are you typically late paying your bills and unfazed by minor inconveniences? A lenient landlord might better suit you, but understand that if she's cutting you slack, she'll probably expect you to be patient when it comes to repairs or other requests.

THEY'RE JUST PLAIN NICE.

Nobody's perfect. But you won't feel confident interacting with a landlord who makes you feel unsafe or disrespected. And that means you won't enjoy your new home. Get a sense of a prospective landlord's temperament by talking with current or previous tenants, if you can, and by speaking or meeting with the landlord a few times, if possible. Does he complain excessively about the previous tenants? Is he intimidating? Does he ask intrusive questions or make offensive comments? Does he fail to listen to what you have to say or answer your questions directly? Remember that a landlord is probably on his best, most professional behavior when interviewing prospective tenants. If the behavior seems neither good nor professional, it's not likely to get much better.

the red tape

Yes, we know. All you really want to do is start holding up paint chips to the walls and shopping for a shag pile throw rug for the bedroom. No one actually likes all the shuffling of papers and crunching of numbers that come first, but everyone has to trudge through the process. With this simple overview of what's involved, at least it'll loom less large.

anatomy of a lease

A lease outlines a contract between a tenant and a landlord. It can be a few lines long or fill several pages. You should read every word of it before adding your signature at the end. It's a legally binding document, and your signature indicates your voluntary agreement to its terms.

A standard apartment lease includes the tenant's name, length of stay (starting and ending dates), the payments involved and when and how they're to be made, and the responsibilities of tenant and landlord. Leases typically also note what utilities are available, eviction clauses, whether or not the space can be sublet (rented to another party by the tenant), rules concerning pets and guests, and liabilities. The address of the residence should also appear, along with contact information for the manager. A lease should always be signed by each tenant and the landlord.

If you don't agree with any of the terms of the lease, discuss them with the landlord. He or she may be willing to waive or alter a policy that makes you uncomfortable. Ink in a note on the lease indicating the waiver or spelling out the new rule, then be sure both you and the landlord initial beside it. Oral contracts are legal in many places, but written leases are preferable, so everyone has a record.

UNDER THE TERMS...

Once you've read the lease carefully and signed on the dotted line, stash it in a safe place. You're responsible for following through on your part of all its terms. Likewise, there are several things your landlord is responsible for and entitled to do.

■ A landlord is responsible for providing a livable and safe home for the tenant. This includes, but is not limited to, ensuring the space passes building, health, and safety codes; installing locks and security devices; and making utility service available.

■ A landlord should have adequate insurance, because he or she can be held liable for crimes, fires, and health risks at the rental property. Renter's insurance purchased by the tenant may cover losses the landlord's policy does not.

■ A landlord may enter a rental to handle repairs, to show the space to potential renters, or, in some cases, if the renter has left for more than seven days. But a landlord must give a tenant notice in advance. Though terms vary, the tenant's permission is always required for non-emergency visits by a landlord.

security deposits
(AND GETTING THEM BACK)

When a landlord asks for a security deposit, don't take it personally. It's a standard way landlords protect themselves financially against tenants who are destructive or irresponsible. If you're neither, you'll get your deposit back when you move out. If, instead, the landlord proposes to withhold part or all of your deposit, he or she has to provide an itemized list of reasons why.

There are two general instances in which a landlord can legally retain a security deposit. One is if a tenant moves out before the lease is up. A landlord can then keep the deposit to cover the unexpected loss of rental income. (Often, however, if you have a new renter lined up, you can move out early and still take your deposit with you.) The other is in the case of damage, which is different from normal wear and tear. Fading and minor dirt or spots on a carpet are normal wear. Cigarette burns, rips, and pet stains are damage. Pinholes in walls are normal wear. Those that require patching and repainting are typically considered damage. Leaving personal property in a rental after you've moved out is even a form of damage, and a landlord can use your deposit money to have it hauled away.

If you and your landlord find yourselves quibbling over the damage issue, you may need to go to a local housing resource agency to find out about your area's ordinances. They'll spell out specifics, such as what qualifies as leaving an apartment unreasonably unclean. They'll also have guidelines that say water damage from plants, open windows, or stopped-up toilets is the tenant's responsibility, but leaks from roofs are the landlord's, and so on.

The best way to protect yourself from false or mistaken damage claims by your landlord is to tour the rental together prior to your moving in (that's where the pencil and paper we mentioned earlier come in handy) and again when you're moving out. Some landlords even have a checklist they use as a part of these tours. Before moving in, make a list of all existing damage on surfaces and appliances within the rental and throughout any exterior area you'll be using (porch, garage, etc.). Be thorough. Both you and the landlord should date and sign the document and keep a copy, then refer back to it during your moving-out tour.

renter's insurance

If you can't afford to replace your belongings if your apartment is struck by a tornado, fire, hurricane, flood, or a burglary, you might want to consider a renter's insurance policy. Your landlord should maintain insurance on the property, but if he or she doesn't—or if your losses don't exceed the deductible—you'll have to sue (and win) to be compensated for them.

A good insurance agent can answer your questions about renter's insurance (start with the person who already handles your auto insurance, if you have it, or any other coverage you have). The agent will ask you for a list of your valuables, from audiovisual equipment to furniture and jewelry, then give you an estimate on what it would cost to insure them, list your choices on deductible amounts, and tell you what documentation would be required to collect on the policy. The agent can also tell you whether you might qualify for any type of discount. Then, it's up to you to get quotes from another agent or two, check you own finances, factor in any advice you might decide to seek from savvy friends or relatives, and decide whether renter's insurance is for you.

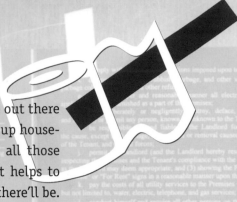

budgeting for basics

As you may have noticed, there are all kinds of people out there making a living off the fact that you've decided to set up house-keeping. While you can't do much to avoid writing all those checks to landlords, power companies, and others, it helps to have a general idea ahead of time how many of them there'll be.

RENT

Expect rent to eat up a third of your monthly income. Yes, one-third. Housing is the most costly routine expense for people in developed nations. (The upside is that we residents of developed nations also have leisure time for activities such as reading books about decorating first apartments.)

Most landlords will ask for the first and last month's rent plus a security deposit before giving you the keys to your new place. That totals approximately three months of rental fees you'll need to have available when you sign the lease. If that little fact suddenly puts the apartment of your dreams out of your range, remember that rental prices can vary greatly within a community. Sometimes a single block divides exorbitant from economical. If the price is right, go ahead and take a look at an apartment in a neighborhood or on a street you're unfamiliar with. The area and property may very well suit your standards. Also keep in mind that prices fluctuate along with the economy. You can sometimes successfully ask for a reduction of the advertised rent during a local recession.

If you still can't afford what you find—or you're willing to sacrifice privacy for savings—get a roommate. A place that's big enough for two will be more expensive overall (unless one of you agrees to sleep in the bathtub), but sharing it with a financially responsible roommate can reduce housing expenses for each of you by a third or more. (If the two of you get along, all the better. For tips on what to look for in a roommate, see page 58.)

UTILITIES

If you've become accustomed to light, heat, running water, and other such creature comforts, then you need to budget for these costs, too. Utilities, which include electricity, telephone service, natural gas or oil, water, and sewer service, typically aren't included in an apartment's rent. In addition to monthly bills, there's a charge for turning on utilities, and deposits are required for new accounts. Some companies will waive your deposit if a customer in good standing (a friend who already has an account, for example) agrees to co-sign on your account. Just be aware that, under this arrangement, any late payments on your bill and the subsequent fees are charged to your friend's account.

Heating and cooling costs are the most expensive utility bills most renters pay, so ask about the space's energy sources, and find out how well insulated the space is. Well-maintained gas furnaces and whole-house air conditioning systems are generally more efficient than electric baseboard for heat or box fans for cooling. High-quality insulation in walls, floors, and ceilings combined with air-tight, insulating-glass windows and solid exterior doors that close snugly translate into energy and money saved. If you can't hold out for the ideal heating and cooling situation, weigh the pros and cons of each residence you look at.

FURNISHINGS

Don't omit the cost of basic furnishings—plus a bit of decorating—from your budget calculations. This isn't just shelter, it's your living space, your very own part of the world. Your days will begin and end here, and so will your moods.

You don't have to furnish and accessorize everything at once. Start small. Make a list of what you have. Make a list of what you need and want. Then start by lining up the essentials—a bed, a chair, a surface for eating. To figure out what your priorities are next, ask yourself some questions. You'll walk your floors each day. Can you live with them the way they are for now, or are you dying to curl your toes in a fluffy rug? You'll see the same windows every day, too. Are the basic white blinds they sport now okay, or are gauzy curtains going to be your first decorating purchase? Give some thought, too, to inexpensive changes you can make to your new living space itself within the terms of your lease. It's amazing how much just a paint job or some new lighting fixtures can perk it up.

Once you have enough basic furnishings to make your home functional, you can add the rest—plants, coffee table, bookshelves, throw pillows—gradually. Budget a small amount to spend monthly, or tackle one room at a time.

EXTRAS

Can't exist without cable television? Want multiple telephone lines to separate work and personal calls or to accommodate multiple roommates? How about a fiber optic Internet connection or a cable Internet service? These are extras that are rarely included in rental fees. Assess their value to you and your lifestyle, and allocate money for them as you would any other housing cost. Be sure to also include the cost of buying and maintaining necessary equipment and/or making monthly payments for services.

the layout

Imagine your first few moments as a new apartment dweller—turning your very own key in your very own lock, and entering an empty expanse that's all yours. Then it hits you. A completely bare room can be a tad intimidating—especially with four or five friends standing beside you, each one holding something heavy and asking where you want it.

make a floor plan

Grab a tape measure and measure the perimeters of the rooms you want to make plans for. (Your land-lord may even let you into your apartment-to-be briefly before you take over the lease, just to record the measurements.) Then, use a pencil and a ruler to transfer a scaled-down version of each room to a sheet of graph paper—that's the paper with little squares on it that you can buy anyplace that sells office supplies. The squares on graph paper are typically ¼ inch (6mm), so the easiest way to create a scaled-down floor plan is to let each ¼-inch line on the paper rep-resent one linear foot (30.5cm) of actual wall space in the apartment. Once you've got the walls marked, draw in scaled versions of win-dows, doors, and any other ele-ments you'll have to work around, such as a fireplace, if you're lucky, or radiators, and label them.

Time to impart a logical but often overlooked moving-in tip: sliding tiny pieces of cutout furniture around a drawing of your apartment's layout is so much more fun than dragging bookcases and futon frames from one spot to another, hoping that eventually the scrambled puzzle of furniture and cardboard boxes will work itself out. As compulsive as it sounds, plotting what goes where on a piece of paper before you start unloading the rented truck is actually the easy way out. Here's how.

create furniture cutouts

On another piece of graph paper, use the same scale—¼ inch equals 1 foot (6mm equals 30.5cm)—to make tiny versions of all the furni-ture pieces you plan to move into your rooms. Cut them out, use markers to give them some color, so they'll stand out against the white floor plans, and label each piece.

start moving

Now, in the comfort of a friend's kitchen, your favorite coffee shop, or any other spot with a flat surface, you can experiment with all kinds of furniture configurations without ever putting on a pair of work gloves or remembering to lift with your legs, not your back.

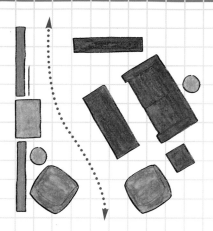

FOLLOWING ARE A FEW POINTERS.

Figure out the focal point for each room—the place around which you want to orient everything else. Most rooms have a logical one: a huge window with a great view, the blank wall where you plan to hang the canvases a friend painted for you or against which you're going to situate the television and VCR.

Play around with your big pieces of furniture first: the couch, the desk, the bed. You'll have fewer places where they'll fit, so it's best to settle them first. Also, their location will typically tell you where other items—the coffee table, the nightstand, etc.—need to go.

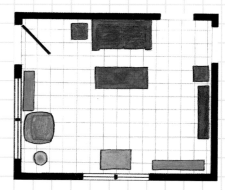

Don't hug the wall. For some reason, lots of first-time furniture arrangers have the idea that shoving most of their furniture up against the walls, so they have maximum floor space, is good. But actually, it often makes your furniture pieces around the rim of the room look isolated and that open floor space in the center seem a little strange. We're not saying sound systems and floor-to-ceiling bookshelves should float in the middle of the room, but some items, such as armchairs and end tables, often look better with a bit of space around them and maybe a floor lamp or plant stand behind them.

Once you've moved a few furniture pieces out into the room, start playing with different angles. Not everything must be parallel or perpendicular to a wall. Experiment with diagonals and with circular and triangular groupings that'll make interaction more comfortable when you have others over.

In the midst of all this experimenting, don't lose sight of the fact that function is at least as important as form. If the arrangement looks great but makes it impossible to see the television from the couch, what's the point? You are going to be living in this space, after all. Think about what kinds of things you'll be doing in each room, then make sure your furniture configuration supports them.

One of the most common activities you and others will carry out in your apartment is walking from one spot to another. Give some thought to what those standard walking routes will be—stove to table, chair to door—and make sure your furniture plan doesn't put a huge piece in the middle of a popular path. Keep those pathways wide enough, too; 2½ feet (76.2 cm) is about the minimum comfortable width.

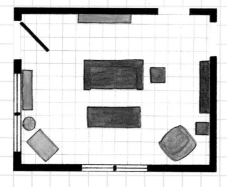

This is also a good time to think about arranging your furniture so it not only makes the most of the features that caused you to fall in love with your apartment, but helps disguise its less-lovable quirks.

IT'S TINY. *Small is beautiful* becomes the buoying mantra of many first-apartment dwellers. If you're making the most of a one-room place or a studio apartment, you've got two workable options. One is to keep the furniture arrangement as open and spacious as possible—the eating and cooking area blending seamlessly with the sitting and sleeping areas. The other is to visually section off one area from another, using furniture such as bookcases, filing cabinets, or even long, narrow tables and couches as dividers. If your landlord will let you mount items on the walls, you can also gain space by trading in freestanding pieces. Sell the bookcase, for example, and buy brackets and shelves instead.

IT'S DARK. If the apartment doesn't get good light, position lamps in the darkest corners. If you've got a choice, go with lamps that have minimal, translucent shades rather than heavy, dark ones. You can also hang mirrors strategically, so they reflect light into darker areas.

IT'S BORING. Maybe the best way to describe your apartment is "boxy": four walls with identical dimensions, and a floor and ceiling to match. Rather than play into the cube-like environment, break it up by setting your furniture off center and at angles, using rugs to split the floor into more interesting sections, and covering one wall completely with a tapestry or hanging mural.

IT'S DESIGNED FOR SHORT PEOPLE. If, even though you'd never make a basketball team, your ceilings feel as if they're caving in on you, arrange some of your lamps so they tilt upward, casting as much light on the ceiling as possible, and draw sightlines downward with interesting rugs, floor cushions, potted plants, and other low-to-the-ground pieces.

sprucing up

Because you're only temporarily renting someone else's property when you lease an apartment, you have two things to consider when it comes to transforming it into the home of your dreams.

One is how much you're willing to invest in fixing up something you're eventually going to leave behind. You won't benefit long-term from devoting all kinds of time and resources to an elaborate faux-finish paint job on every wall. Then again, if a sunnier color in the kitchen is going to lift your spirits for the next 365 days or so, it's worth repainting it. There are also plenty of simple sprucing-up jobs you can do—then undo and take with you when you go, such as changing the handles on the bathroom cabinets to ones that aren't quite so 1970s, or adding interesting finials (those stoppers on the ends) to the personality-deprived curtain rods in the bedroom.

The other consideration is how much your landlord will allow you to do. Every situation is different. Some landlords have a strict policy against allowing tenants to paint or wallpaper. Others, especially if their rental property is an older building or converted house, are much more lenient. Some have a group of colors for all the apartments in a building, and they'll allow you to repaint if you use a color in that mix. Others are so thrilled that you want to add value to the apartment by giving a few of the rooms fresh coats of paint or wallpaper borders that they'll buy the supplies if you do the work.

Once you know how much you're willing and able to take on, here are the do-it-yourself basics you need to know.

painting walls

One of the easiest and least expensive ways to brighten a dingy room or give a dull one character (not to mention your personal stamp) is to splash a fresh paint color on the walls.

PAINT

You've got two general types of paint to choose from: oil-based (alkyd) and water-based (latex). In most cases, latex is the way to go. Though alkyd paints may be slightly more damage resistant, latex paints today are plenty durable. They're also nontoxic, quick-drying, and they clean up with soap and water as opposed to mineral spirits. The only time you might want to use alkyd paints instead is if you plan to also coat doors, window trim, or other accent spots that'll need a hard finish.

When you buy your paint, the salesperson will ask you what sort of gloss you want. The level of gloss affects the shine and brightness of your walls.

FLAT PAINTS, the most common kind for walls and ceilings, are easy on the eye, reflect little light, reduce glare, and help hide small imperfections.

EGGSHELL, LO-LUSTRE, and **SATIN PAINTS** are good for heavy-use areas that will be subjected to frequent washings—maybe walls around the kitchen counter and stove. They have a slight sheen and hold up a bit better than flat paints.

SEMIGLOSS PAINTS have a slightly greater sheen and can handle a bit more wear and tear than satin paints.

GLOSS and **HIGH-GLOSS PAINTS,** also called enamels, dry to an extremely shiny finish, making them better for woodwork and furniture than entire walls. An enamel surface can withstand heavy use and scrubbing, but it will also reflect any surface imperfection.

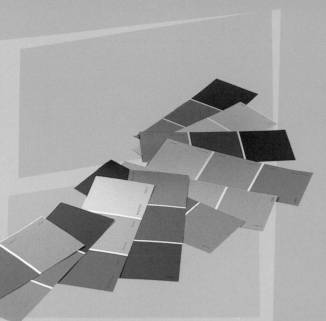

ESTIMATING QUANTITY

To figure out how much paint you need, measure the perimeter of your room. Multiply the result by the ceiling height to get the total square feet or meters you need to cover with paint. Don't worry about deducting the space taken up by windows and doors unless they add up to more than 100 square feet (9 square m), which is unlikely in an apartment. Divide your total square feet or meters into the number of square feet or meters your paint can promises to cover. Round up to the nearest whole number to determine how many cans you need.

CHOOSING COLORS

First, head to the paint store toting along whatever you want your paint to match or contrast with—a color you clipped from a magazine, a cushion from your couch, one of your electric-green martini glasses. Pick out a bunch of strips of sample colors, and take everything back home. Tack the samples in place on the wall, and pay attention to how they look at different times of day and under different lighting conditions. Start narrowing your choices until you eventually pick the one you'd most like to see in large quantities 24 hours a day. If you simply can't decide—or you're super compulsive—you can always choose two or three paint colors, buy the smallest amount available of each, and apply the paints to scraps of wood. Live with your larger color samples for a day or two before deciding which one you'll use to cover the whole room, remembering that the larger the final painted area, the stronger the color will seem. For a few more tips on choosing colors, see Color Your World, page 108.

MATERIALS & TOOLS

BRUSHES. Nylon or polyester brushes are best for latex paints. Use a natural-bristle brush with alkyd paints. Whichever bristle type you pick, you want brushes with contoured tops that form an oval or a rounded edge. They're best for cutting a fine line along trim and at corners where walls and ceilings meet.

DROP CLOTHS. Disposable plastic drop cloths protect flooring and furniture from paint splatters.

PAINT ROLLERS. Choose a roller with a heavy wire frame and a sturdy, threaded handle that extends (making it possible to easily reach the high spots). The painting surface of the roller is also called a sleeve or cover. It slides on and off the roller cage so you can clean and store it. The length of the nap on sleeves or covers varies; the more irregular your wall surface, the longer nap you'll need.

PRIMER. This specially formulated paint adheres well to bare surfaces and provides an inexpensive base for your more expensive topcoat to stick to.

ROLLER PAN. You need a shallow metal pan with a ramp. You'll run your roller up and down the ramp to evenly distribute the paint on the sleeve.

TRIM GUARD. Also called an edger, this handy hand-held tool lets you shield adjacent surfaces such as window glass or carpeting from the fresh paint you're applying to a wall. It's not essential, but it's a nice-to-have extra.

GENERAL TECHNIQUES

PREP YOUR WALLS. You can paint right over just about any surface, just quickly sponge off any dirt, dust, or mildew first, and let it dry. Also, remove the covers on electrical receptacles, light switches, heating grates, or plate covers from your walls, so you won't splatter them or coat their edges. Cover electrical outlets with masking tape.

PRIME. Apply a coat of primer with a roller or brush. Choose the type that's right for your job; latex primers are for bare wood, others are designed for sheetrock or plaster. Make sure your primer coat is completely dry before you move on.

PAINT. Two simple guidelines will make your paint job a success (and the process more fun): work from top to bottom; and outline first, then fill in second. If you're painting the room's ceiling in addition to the walls, start there. Move on to the walls, and end with door and window trim, doors, and finally baseboards. Use a brush first to outline all the areas a roller can't reach, such as corners, places where the wall meets trim, etc. When you're ready to roll, precondition your roller sleeve by rinsing it with water and spinning it until it's dry. (You don't need to precondition a lamb's-wool sleeve.) Fill one third of your paint tray with paint, load the roller in the deep end of the tray, and smooth it on the sloping end to evenly distribute the paint. Start at the top third of your walls, and work your way down, applying equal pressure and spreading the paint evenly. It's helpful to lay the paint on in the shape of an M or W, then fill in the blank spaces, working from the unpainted areas into the wet paint.

GENERAL TECHNQUES

PREP YOUR FLOOR. Your floor must be free of any gloss or sheen before you apply the paint. Use the floor polisher to buff away the top surface and remove any dirt or grit in the process. When you're finished, use the vacuum to clean up your mess, focusing special attention on cracks and crevices between floorboards.

MARK YOUR PATTERN (optional). If you're painting a design, map it out on graph paper first. Then, use measuring tools and a pencil to transfer the pattern to your floor. If your design features straight lines (a checkerboard pattern, for example), you can use a chalk line to snap the lines according to evenly spaced marks on the edges of the floor.

PAINT. Start by using a brush to outline the perimeter of the floor and to fill in any wide spaces or cracks between floorboards. Once you've got the edges painted, use the roller to fill in the rest of the floor. Working on an area that's about 24 inches (61 cm) wide at a time, paint the entire length of your floorboards, from one wall to the other, then move over to the next strip. Using the edge of a board as your stopping and starting point keeps your wet edge of paint on an even plane rather than in the middle of a board, where lap marks would be visible. Let your floor dry completely between coats if you're adding more than one. For added durability, finish with a couple of coats of matte-finish, non-yellowing polyurethane.

painting floors

If your new place features a wooden floor that's seen better days—or that the previous tenant painted magenta to match her beaded curtains—and your landlord is agreeable, you have the perfect canvas for applying your own color and design.

MATERIALS & TOOLS

BRUSHES & ROLLER. The same painting tools you use on walls will work on floors.

FLOOR POLISHER. Tool-rental outlets and even the floor-care centers of many grocery stores rent polishers you can use to roughen up the surface of your floor.

VACUUM CLEANER. You need one to do what it does best: remove dirt and dust, plus sanding residue. A tack rag (basically sticky cheesecloth designed to pick up dust) is a more labor-intensive substitute.

PAINT

The folks at your local paint store should be able to help you choose the paint best suited for the type and condition of your wood floor. For high-traffic, heavy-use floors, oil-based enamels offer the best durability. You can also find oil-based paint formulated especially for floors and porches, though it's available in only a limited range of colors.

wallpapering

When you want to establish a definite look—art deco, Asian tea room, 1960s retro—wallpaper, with its wealth of patterns and styles, is much more effective than paint. It's also better at hiding flaws in imperfect walls. The downside is that hanging it is a bit more challenging than rolling on paint, but there's nothing so tricky you can't master it.

WALLPAPER TYPES

Save grass cloth, delicate handmade papers, and wall coverings made from pure silk for the home you buy after your trust fund comes through. For now, vinyl wall coverings are more affordable and durable.

PAPER-BACKED VINYL is not only washable and sturdy, it also typically comes in an easy-to-apply prepasted form. Best of all, paper-backed vinyl is available in tons of patterns and in textures ranging from leatherlike to embossed.

FABRIC-BACKED VINYL is a bit more durable than paper-backed vinyl, but it's typically not prepasted.

VINYL-COATED PAPER is the least expensive option, but it's also the least durable. Grease splatters, beverage spills, and the like will leave permanent marks.

MATERIALS & TOOLS

BUCKET & SPONGE. You'll use these as you hang your paper to remove any wallpaper paste oozing from the edges of your newly applied paper.

LADDER. An obvious necessity if you're papering from ceiling to floor.

LEVEL. Anytime you need to determine a straight vertical or horizontal line on your walls, you'll need a level.

PAINT ROLLER OR PASTE BRUSH. If you're not working with prepasted wallpaper, you'll need one of these tools to apply adhesive to the back of your paper.

PLUMB LINE. Simply a weight attached to the end of a string, this tool helps you establish a straight, vertical layout line. Tie the string to a nail near the top of the wall so the weight is just above the floor. When the line stops swinging, align a ruler with the string to mark your layout line.

UTILITY KNIFE. Use a knife with breakaway blades to trim off excess paper at ceiling and floor molding, light fixtures, etc.

SCISSORS. You'll use them to cut your wallpaper strips to size.

SEAM ROLLER. A seam roller is indispensable when it comes to pressing down the seams where two pieces of wallpaper meet.

SMOOTHING BRUSH. The flexible bristles on this brush help you smooth your hung paper so it's free of bubbles and wrinkles.

TAPE MEASURE. When you're measuring and cutting your paper, you've got to have one.

TRIM GUIDE. A painting edger or a broad knife can serve as a trim guide. You'll use it to press your wet wallpaper into a ceiling or wall joint before you trim it.

WATER TRAY. If you're using prepasted wallpaper, you'll need to soak it before hanging it.

ESTIMATING QUANTITY

Using the same system described for estimating the quantity of paint (page 23), figure the total square feet or meters of your room's wall space. Divide your total by the square feet or meters a roll of the wallpaper you've chosen promises to cover. You probably won't come out with an even number; round up to determine how many rolls you should buy.

Go figure: Nobody knows why, but although wallpaper is *priced* by the single roll, it's *sold* only in packages of double rolls—a good thing to know when you're estimating how much you need to buy.

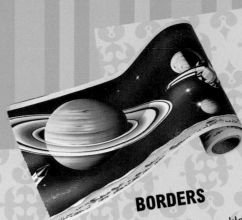

BORDERS

Not ready to tackle an entire wall? Hanging a border is an excellent (and easy) way to test your interest in wallpapering—and it may add all the decorative accent you need. Borders come in all kinds of patterns and various widths for hanging around windows, doors, mirrors, and the tops of walls.

GENERAL TECHNIQUES

PREP YOUR WALLS. Give your walls a good washing down and dry them well, patch any holes or cracks with wall compound, and, after the compound is dry, sand the patched areas until they're smooth. Also, remove the covers on electrical receptacles and light switches, cover electrical outlets with masking tape, and remove any heating grates or plate covers from your walls. If you like to follow all the rules, apply a coat of primer to your walls. Primer is only a must if you're papering over new drywall, but it'll promote adhesion on any type of wall. Finally, apply a coat of wallpaper sizing, a treatment that makes your walls tacky so the wallpaper paste or adhesive has some- thing to bond with.

HANG THE PAPER. Use a level or plumb line to lay out a straight, vertical starting point on your wall. Cut your first strip of wallpaper from the roll. You want your strip a little longer than your wall is tall; you'll trim it later. Soak your strip in water, following your paper manufacturer's instructions, or apply wallpaper paste to the strip. Position the strip at the ceiling joint of the wall, leaving a few extra inches at the top, and carefully align one side with your starting line. Use your hands and the smoothing brush to smooth the strip in place, starting at the top and working down. Once the strip is straight, continue brushing to remove any wrinkles or bubbles. Hang subsequent strips the same way, carefully aligning the seams and using the seam roller to press them in place. As you go, use a wet sponge to wipe up any paste that oozes out of the seams.

TRIM. Where your wallpaper strips meet the ceiling, floor, or any trim, hold the trim guide in the joint, and use the razor knife to cut away the excess paper.

hanging curtains & blinds

Whether your motivation is privacy, decoration, or blocking the sun that streams into your bedroom far too early on Saturday morning, hanging some sort of covering over your windows will likely be one of your first sprucing-up activities.

curtains

MEASURING FOR CURTAINS

Two basic measurements will tell you what size curtains you need.

■ The length of your curtain rod tells you how wide your curtains should be.

■ The length from the mounted rod to the windowsill (for sill-length curtains) or the floor (for floor-length curtains) tells you how long. For this second measurement, measure from the rod itself for curtains with a casing that will be threaded onto the rod; measure from the base of a curtain ring, if you're using rings. For sill-length curtains, deduct ⅜ inch (9.5mm) from the measurement, so the curtains will clear the sill comfortably, or add 2 to 4 inches (5.1 to 10.2 cm), so they'll hang just below the sill. For floor-length curtains, again, deduct ⅜ inch (9.5mm) from the length for clearance, or add 2 to 8 inches (5.1 to 20.3 cm), and let your curtains puddle on the floor.

HANGING THE ROD

The windows in your apartment will probably already be outfitted with rods for hanging curtains. If not—or if you want to replace an existing rod with one you like better— simply center the rod over the window. Place it about 4 inches (10.2 cm) above the top of the window, and make sure it extends an equal amount on either side of the window. Rods typically come packaged with the hardware and easy instructions you need to attach them to the wall.

blinds

MEASURING FOR BLINDS

You can mount most blinds on the window trim, on the wall outside the window frame, or inside of the window's recess, which needs to be at least 1¼ inch (3.2 cm) deep. Decide which option you want, then measure your window. Measure the width at the top, middle, and bottom of the window (warped wood around the windows can affect the width); if the dimensions differ, use the smallest one. Also, measure the length of the window, so you choose a blind with the correct extension amount.

HANGING BLINDS

Blinds come with mounting brackets, most of which have predrilled holes on both ends and on the back. You'll use only one set of holes, depending on which of the three places you're mounting them.

■ Position the brackets where you want them, and lightly mark where you'll screw through the appropriate predrilled holes.

■ Drill pilot holes where you made the marks.

■ Use a screwdriver to install the brackets with screws (typically packaged with the brackets).

■ Push the blind's header bar into the brackets.

■ If necessary, snip the blind cords so your blinds are the proper length; directions for doing so are usually included with the blinds.

 Make sure your landlord approves any drilling in the walls necessary to mount window treatments in your apartment.

fixing up furniture

Unlike walls and floors, tables, chairs, and their counterparts are pieces you will take with you when your lease is up and you move on (assuming you're not renting a furnished apartment). That makes them an especially good focus for your fixing-up time and resources.

painting furniture

Brushing on fresh paint is the easiest way to give a piece of furniture a new look. You can start with already-painted furniture or with new pieces of unfinished furniture. Flea markets, yard sales, and relatives' attics are great sources for the former. Stores that specialize in unpainted furniture offer a wide selection of the latter, though they're often much pricier than used pieces.

If you're investing in unfinished furniture you plan to have around for awhile, solid-wood pieces are the best choice. While you can find unfinished furniture made of particle board, plywood, and veneers, solid-wood construction is stronger and longer lasting. Depending on where you purchase your unfinished furniture, it can come either assembled or unassembled. If it's unassembled, it should be accompanied by illustrated instructions and all the hardware you need to easily put your piece together.

PAINT

Just as when you're painting walls, you've got a choice between oil-based (alkyd) and water-based (latex) paints and flat, semigloss, and gloss sheens. Again, the advantage of latex paints is that they're nearly odorless, they clean up with soap and water, and they dry quickly. Alkyd paints, on the other hand, are more resistant to wear and tear. For added color options, you may also want to experiment with artist's acrylics, sold in tubes or jars. They're great for painting small areas, detailing a motif, outlining, and highlighting. Artist's acrylics are more concentrated than household paint, so you may want to thin them with water before using them.

FURNITURE-PAINTING MATERIALS & TOOLS

BRUSHES. You probably don't need to invest in specialized decorative painting brushes. A 2-inch (5.1 cm) or 3-inch (7.6 cm) flat paintbrush used for household painting is versatile enough to handle most jobs. A straight-edge brush works well on flat surfaces; an angled brush will be handier when you want to paint clean, straight lines and nice sharp corners. For detail work such as outlining, highlighting, or blending, you'll want a selection of small artist's brushes.

CARBON or **GRAPHITE TRANSFER PAPER.** You'll need this if you're transferring a design to the surface of your furniture.

GLAZE MEDIUM. Formulated to dry more slowly than paint, glaze medium gives you a longer working time for techniques that call for manipulation of the top coat of paint, such as rag rolling or stippling. It comes in either water- or oil-based formulas and dries clear.

DROP CLOTHS. They provide a protective layer between your painting project and your floor. Use an old sheet, purchase an inexpensive plastic cloth, or spread out old newspapers.

RAGS. Lint-free rags are indispensable when it comes to wiping up drips and spills and for cleaning your brushes.

SANDPAPER. Sandpaper is categorized by its grade (coarse, medium, fine, and extra fine) or by a number that indicates the amount of grit used per square inch on the sanding surface (#150 to #200 are considered medium grade, for example).

PRIMERS. If you're working on unfinished furniture, you need a primer to fill and seal the bare wood so the surface will better accept your paint. Choose a good all-purpose primer-sealer formulated for use with water- or oil-based paints.

TACK CLOTH. You'll use this sticky cloth to clean your wood's surface, removing debris and sanding residue before you paint.

VARNISHES & PROTECTIVE COATS. If you want to give your painted surface extra protection, add sheen, or tone down a too-shiny surface, you can apply a few top coats of clear varnish or polyurethane. Varnishes come in water- and oil-based formulas and in sheens ranging from matte to high-gloss.

WOOD FILLER. If your piece features small dents or nicks, natural flaws, or nail or staple holes, use wood filler to even the surface before applying your primer or first coat of paint.

GENERAL TECHNIQUES

Whether you're painting unfinished or already-painted furniture, try to work in a space that's free of drafts and airborne dirt, so specks of dust and lint will be less likely to land on your just-painted surfaces.

PAINTING UNFINISHED FURNITURE

1. Fill any holes or indentations with wood filler, following the manufacturer's instructions for application and drying time.

2. Once the filler is dry, use a fine-grit sandpaper to remove any excess filler and to buff your entire piece.

3. Use the tack cloth to remove any sanding debris.

4. Seal the wood with a coat of primer. Once it's dry, sand again, and again use the tack cloth to remove any debris.

5. Apply your first coat of paint, let it dry, sand your piece again, and wipe it clean.

6. Add your top coat, let it dry, then finish with several coats of varnish if you like.

PAINTING ALREADY-PAINTED FURNITURE

If the existing paint on your piece of furniture is in good condition, just sand the piece thoroughly with medium-grade sandpaper, and apply your new paint. If it features a few chips and cracks, sand the damaged areas smooth before painting. For pieces with more damaged existing paint, use wood filler to even out the nicks and gaps, let it dry, sand it smooth, then apply a coat of primer before adding your paint. It's a good idea, in this case, to apply two coats of your finish paint, sanding between the first and second coat.

SPECIAL FINISHES & DECORATIVE TECHNIQUES

Here are some easy options for adding texture, pattern, and splashes of colorful design to your painted furniture.

WEATHERING

It doesn't have to make sense—some of us simply want our brand-new pieces to look old. Using two paint colors, first paint on a base coat of your lighter color, and let it dry completely. Then use one of the following approaches to "age" your piece.

■ Mix the darker shade of paint with water, and stir well. You'll need to experiment with the ratio of water to paint. For a very thin color wash, use more water. Paint a wash of the darker color over the entire surface of the wood. Allow the paint to sit for a few minutes, then wipe some of the paint away with a clean rag to give it an uneven or weathered appearance. For more color, give the piece a second wash.

■ Apply the darker paint to a paintbrush. Offload the brush onto a rag until it's almost dry. Paint the piece with the almost-dry brush, dragging the tip of the brush in long strokes until the piece is entirely covered. Apply several almost-dry coats in this fashion, building up the layers of top color.

■ Paint the entire piece with the darker paint. Allow the paint to dry thoroughly. Use fine-grit sandpaper to lightly sand away some of the darker color to reveal the lighter shade underneath. Sand very lightly to prevent exposing the raw wood.

STENCILING

Stenciling is simply painting through a hole (or pattern of holes) cut in a piece of stencil material that you've taped against your surface. All you need is a stencil (the pattern of cutout holes), paint (acrylic is most common; specialty stencil paints, paint sticks, and crayons are also available), and a tool for applying the color (artist's brushes, stencil brushes, and sponges are all options). Precut stencils in every design motif imaginable are available at craft stores. You can also design your own stencils and cut them out of a water-resistant material, such as acetate.

1. Use painter's tape or spray adhesive to fix your stencils in place.

2. Dab on paint to fill the stencil's cutout area. Different brushing techniques produce different effects.

> **DRY-BRUSH** application, which involves blotting your brush on a paper towel before applying the paint, creates a soft, muted result.

> **STIPPLING,** or applying the paint in a quick up-and-down motion, creates a fine, textural effect.

> **SWIRLING,** a method of applying a small amount of paint in a downward, twisting motion, creates a smooth finish with dark and light gradations.

Don't ever drag your brush over the stencil; you risk driving paint under the stencil and outside the design's border.

3. Gently remove the stencils, being careful not to smudge the painted design as you do.

SPONGING

Sponging is one of the simplest ways to texturize a surface with paint—a little dipping, a little patting, and you've got interesting patches of color that can serve as your final finish or as a background for additional treatments. Sponging is also a versatile technique. Use a soft touch, and the look is luminous. Apply more pressure and contact to intensify the color in specific areas, and you can create different shades of color. Or, blend several colors into each other, and you end up with a graduated effect. You can use sponges to produce uniform design elements, too; cut dots, diamonds, or any other basic shape from sponges, then use them to stamp your surface.

Kitchen sponges, cosmetic sponges, sea sponges, and sponge mitts all create interesting finishes. You can also "sponge" on paint with everything from crumpled newspaper to nubby fabric—all with their own imaginative effects.

STAMPING

A close cousin of sponging, stamping is another nearly effortless way to add painted accents to any surface. Rubber stamps come in an array of sizes and in designs ranging from spirals and stars to all the letters of the alphabet. Simply dip your stamp in acrylic paint, and press it against the surface you want to decorate.

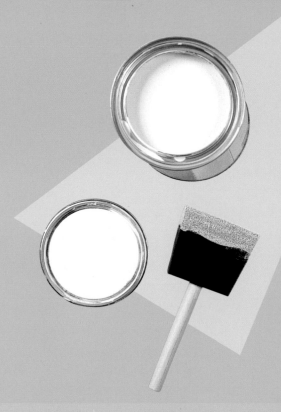

PICKLING

Pickle a piece when you want it to display a satisfyingly sun-bleached look atop visible wood grain.

1. Using steel wool or a wire brush, open up the grain of the wood by brushing firmly in the direction of the grain. Wipe away all dust and residue with a clean rag.

2. Use an old paintbrush to work the latex paint deep into the grain of the wood. Wipe away the excess paint with a clean rag, leaving the paint in the grain and crevices of the wood. Work small areas at a time; the paint dries quickly. Once you've worked the entire surface, allow the paint to dry thoroughly.

3. Lightly sand the entire surface. Remove all residue with a tack or lint-free cloth.

4. For a more natural look, rub furniture wax onto the surface, then buff the piece. For a more durable finish, apply several coats of varnish, lightly sanding in between coats.

refurbishing wood

Lots of times, varnished wooden pieces you pick up at flea markets or tag sales look as if they need a complete overhaul when they'll actually spring back to life with nothing more than a good, old-fashioned cleaning. To make the process sound like more of a job when you're describing it to others, refer to it by its official name: refurbishing.

1. Applying mineral spirits (paint thinner you can buy at any paint or hardware store) is the best way to remove wax, grease, and grime from old wood. Use a clean cotton rag, and if you're working indoors, make sure you've got the windows open to air out the fumes. Also, because the fume buildup can be flammable, it's a good idea to turn off the pilot light of your stove while you're working.

2. Clean small areas at a time, wiping away any residue with a clean, dry cloth as you go.

3. If your piece is really filthy, you may have to give it a second or even third dose of mineral spirits.

4. Once your piece is clean, you can assess it. You may simply see a few spots where its finish has worn off. If so, slip on some rubber gloves, and use a clean sponge or cloth to dab on some matching stain. Once it's dry, give the wood a top coat of clear, wipe-on finish. If, on the other hand, your assessment tells you your piece still looks pretty shabby, read on.

staining stripped or unfinished wood

In addition to the hundreds of paint-chip samples they stock, paint stores also typically have samples of stains, which come in every wood tone imaginable, plus lots of pastels. You want natural wood colors if your goal is to show off the grain of the wood. Pastels are better at masking imperfections.

1. If your furniture is made of pine or another softwood, apply a coat of wood conditioner before you start. Softwoods have uneven grains that make for uneven stain absorption. The conditioner will help even out the stain penetration.

2. Wearing rubber gloves, pour a small amount of stain into an open pan or paint tray.

3. Dip in a clean sponge, cloth, or paintbrush, squeeze out the excess, and apply the stain to a small area in long, continuous strokes, following the grain pattern of the wood.

4. Wipe the wet stain with a clean, dry cloth to even it out.

5. Apply as many coats as you need, depending on how dark you want your stain. When you're finished, apply a top coat of sealer, varnish, shellac, or polyurethane, depending on the look you want.

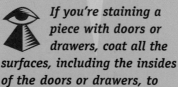 *If you're staining a piece with doors or drawers, coat all the surfaces, including the insides of the doors or drawers, to keep the wood from warping.*

refinishing or stripping wood

Cleaning off a piece of furniture's dirt and dull top layer of finish may not solve other problems, including extensive cracking or peeling of its remaining finish or stains and water damage. You've got two other more work-intensive choices if your piece needs more help: refinishing, which means removing the surface finish and replacing it with another; or full-blown stripping, taking all the finish out until your piece is stripped down to its bare wood, then restaining or painting and finishing.

While neither option is overwhelmingly complicated—and there are now nontoxic, environmentally friendly products on the market, which make the processes and cleanup more pleasant—each does require specific steps and special tools and materials. Buying a simple guide that focuses on refinishing and stripping techniques will be well worth the small expense. It'll walk you through everything from how to choose the right product for the job to tricks for stripping hard-to-clean crevices.

cleaning furniture hardware

Often, the hinges, handles, knobs, and pulls attached to handed-down or salvaged pieces of wood furniture could use some fixing up, too. Use ordinary metal cleaners to clean plated steel pieces. (You can tell they're steel by holding a magnet near one of the pieces; steel attracts magnets.) Clean solid brass, copper, or bronze pieces with brass refurbisher.

1. Apply a thick coat of the refurbisher with a bristle brush.

2. Let it work for about 10 minutes.

3. Wipe off the refurbisher with a clean cloth, apply another coat, if necessary, then buff the cleaned hardware.

removing rust

Wrought-iron outdoor furniture pieces can be transformed into funky indoor accents by cleaning them up and brushing on a coat of paint. If you have a set that's rusting, use a wire brush to remove the loose rust, then lightly sand it or rub it with some fine steel wool dipped in kerosene. Once the kerosene is dry, it's ready to paint.

perking up wicker

Hose off old wicker that looks dusty and tired—a car wash is a good place to do this if you don't have a yard. If your wicker piece needs some extra attention, brush it with a small brush and some dishwashing liquid, then rinse it thoroughly again, and let it dry in the sun. For added life, give your wicker chair or table a thin coat of paint or varnish.

sewing primer

So you didn't win the home economics award in high school. With a simple sewing kit and a few basic techniques, you can reattach buttons and stitch beaded fringe on curtains with the best of them.

the kit

All you really need is an assortment of colored threads, needles of different sizes, and a pair of small, sharp, good quality scissors. In a jam, you'll be glad to find your kit also stocked with a few safety pins, a selection of fasteners such as snaps and hooks and eyes, and buttons in various sizes and colors, particularly white and black. You could also include a thimble (worn on the middle finger to help push needles through thick fabrics), a needle threader, and, if you find yourself cutting lots of lengths of heavy fabric, a large pair of scissors. A tape measure makes measuring soft or curved pieces a cinch. Even if you never pick up a needle, you'll find it useful to have around.

basic stitches

The simplest stitch, a **RUNNING STITCH**, covers lots of ground quickly. Thread a needle and make a knot on one end of the thread. Insert the needle several times through the fabric at evenly spaced intervals, then pull the needle and thread through. Repeat.

A **BACKSTITCH** has more strength than a running stitch. Bring the needle through both layers of fabric you're sewing together, push it back down about 1/8 inch (3mm) in the direction you started from, and pull the thread through completely. Stitch forward the same distance as the first stitch, then backwards 1/8 inch (3mm). Repeat.

Use a **SLIP STITCH** for hems. Make a small fold that just encases the raw edge of the fabric; press it. Make another fold the size you want the hem to be; press again. Put the needle inside the fold, push it through to the front, and pick up just a thread or two when sending the needle back through to the fold. Don't pull the thread too taut, or the fabric will appear puckered. Repeat.

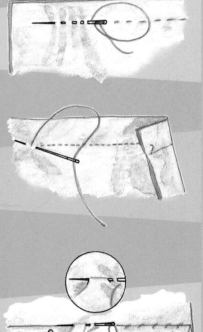

sewing on a button

Putting on a button is a snap, and good sewing practice for beginners. After threading the needle, make a knot with both ends of the thread, so you'll speed up the process by sewing with both strands at once. Hold the button in place, and drive the needle from under the fabric, up through one of the holes, and back down through the opposite hole. Repeat four or five times (more if your fabric is heavy). For added strength, poke the needle back up through the fabric, but not through the button, and wrap around the threads twice. Bring the needle back under the fabric and tie off, cutting off the excess thread.

 *When sewing, use thicker thread and larger needles for heavy fabrics. Likewise, fine needles and thread work better on lightweight fabrics.*

no-sew alternatives

Let's face it, there are going to be times—perhaps all the time—when you're just too busy to hand-stitch a hem on a piece of fabric to create a tablecloth or to whip up homemade curtains. Here are some easy-way-out alternatives.

■ To avoid hemming altogether, use pinking shears. They cut fabric in such a way that it won't fray, and add a decorative edge at the same time. You can also avoid hemming by choosing the right fabric. Some, such as felt, vinyl, ultrasuede, or fleece, won't fray no matter how you cut them.

■ To join two pieces of cloth that won't need frequent washings, try fabric glue. Its downside is that it can make some fabrics a little stiff.

■ For a more permanent and washable solution, use fusible web. When placed between two pieces of fabric and ironed, this white, mesh-like material melts and bonds to the pieces. Just be careful not to touch it directly with the iron, or it will attach itself to your appliance. Fusible web comes in rolls ½ inch (1.3 cm) wide, or on bolts in wider widths.

■ Snaps offer an interesting alternative for holding fabrics together, and even for hemming. It takes a little planning and care to line the halves up correctly, but you'll need only a hammer to set the snaps. Just follow the directions on their packaging.

The baker's-dozen basics you'll need for simple repairs and decorating.

APARTMENT DWELLER'S TOOLBOX

1 | **WORK GLOVES**
They'll prevent calluses and scrapes, and remove the excuse that you can't fix it now because you'll get dirty. Leather and synthetic gloves keep your hands warmer and drier than cotton or canvas.

2 | A 16-ounce (448 g) **CLAW HAMMER**
This is a basic carpenter's tool designed for all-around use. It has a flat side for driving nails and a "claw" on the peen side for removing them. Also, buy a supply of various sizes of nails and tacks.

3 | **PLIERS**
There's a variety of styles and sizes; you'll need two kinds. Long, straight-nosed pliers with side cutters are great for holding on in tight spaces and for snipping wire. Groove-joint pliers, when opened to their maximum of 2 inches (5.1 cm) wide, resemble the monster in *Alien*. Even cooler, they allow you to grip large nuts and fittings when your hands just won't do.

4 | **UTILITY KNIFE**
When scissors won't cut it, a utility knife will, whether you're opening cardboard boxes or trimming wallpaper. Retract the blade when you're not using it.

5 | **COMBINATION SCREWDRIVER**
Keep screws of various sizes handy, too, and you'll use this versatile tool often. Its removable heads accommodate several sizes of standard and Phillips-head screws.

6 | **PUTTY KNIFE**
Just add elbow grease, and this humble tool removes paint, finish, or glue. A flexible 1½-inch (3.8 cm) blade is good for all-around use.

7 | **SOCKET WRENCH SET** with **NUT DRIVER**
A set, with a variety of wrenches and sockets in metric and standard sizes, is most useful. You'll tighten or loosen nuts and bolts on appliances (and vehicles) and be able to reach tight spaces with ease using the ratchet handles and extension shafts.

8 | A retractable 25-foot (7.6 m) **METAL TAPE MEASURE**
Precise measurements are key, whether you're designing your apartment's floor plan or installing shelves.

9 | A 12-inch (30.5 cm) **COMBINATION SQUARE**
It looks like a triangle, measures 45 to 90° angles and short distances, and has a built-in level for keeping things straight. You can use it for everything from hanging pictures to building furniture.

10 | **POWER DRILL** and assorted **DRILL BIT SET**
You'll make up reasons to bore holes or drive screws in wood, metal, and plastic with this tool. A cordless, variable-speed drill with a ⅜-inch (9.5mm) chuck opening is your best bet. (Remember to recharge it after using it.) A more powerful drill will get the job done more quickly and with greater precision. Drills can also convert to sanders and polishers with the proper attachments.

11 | **TOOLBOX SAW**
You can use a small, easy-to-handle handsaw for cutting everything from shelving to plywood.

12 | **GLUE**
Sometimes a drop of the sticky stuff is all you need. White all-purpose glue bonds wood, paper, and cloth, and cleans up with soap and water. Synthetic resin adhesives, also known as epoxies, provide waterproof fastening. Read labels to determine which types you need for different sticking situations.

13 | A can of lightweight **HOUSEHOLD OIL**
A drop of this stops hinges from squeaking, and that makes it worth its weight in gold.

Buy the best quality tools you can afford. Store them together in a toolbox or sturdy basket, always in the same convenient place, so they're both out of the way and accessible.

settling in

No doubt about it, setting up house from scratch can seem overwhelming. You'll brave bewildering expeditions to discount and home accessory stores, spend a lot of money, carry home a lot of heavy bags, then realize you still don't have what you need to open a bottle of wine or dry your hands on something other than a bath towel. The process of settling in becomes much more manageable when you understand that your new home needs a relatively small but essential number of fundamental items to function smoothly. Focus on them first, then add flourishes and embellishments later— or put the extras on your housewarming-party wish list; see page 103.

kitchen

Unless you plan to live entirely on takeout, here are the basics to consider for your kitchen. We'll leave the prioritizing of the extras—from salad spinners and potato mashers to woks and muffin pans—to you.

cookware

12-INCH (30.5 CM) SKILLET. A teflon-coated aluminum skillet, which is affordable, lighter than cast iron, and easy to clean, is a good, all-purpose choice.

STOCKPOT WITH LID. Get one with at least a 6-quart (5.7 L) capacity.

SAUCE PAN WITH LID. One with a 3 to 4-quart (2.9 to 3.8 L) capacity should do.

LARGE COLANDER. Stainless steel has that nice professional-kitchen look, but heavy-duty plastic willl work just fine.

BAKING PAN. A 9 x 12-inch (22.9 x 30.5 cm) rectangle will work for cornbread, brownies, and birthday cakes for friends.

COOKIE SHEET. Round or rectangular; you decide. Either will accommodate nachos, potato skins, and, of course, cookies.

SET OF NESTED BOWLS. Tempered-glass bowls can serve as mixing bowls, refrigerator storage bowls, and serving bowls, plus they're tough enough for a microwave or freezer.

CUTTING BOARD. Plastic is cheaper than wood and (when cleaned) doesn't harbor bacteria. Scrub the board after every use with hot, soapy water. Rinse it with one tablespoon of bleach in a gallon of water.

MEASURING CUPS AND SPOONS. Again, stainless-steel varieties have more flair—especially if they're hanging out on display—but plastic will get the job done.

appliances

BLENDER OR FOOD PROCESSOR. A food processor is more versatile—it purees, grinds, slices, dices, and grates. But a basic blender with only high and low settings will do for most tasks, from mixing smoothies to making pesto.

ELECTRIC MIXER. Freestanding retro-style mixers look funkier, but they also cost a lot more. An inexpensive, hand-held type is plenty sufficient. If you don't plan to bake at all, scratch even the simpler style off your list.

TOASTER OVEN. These convenient multitaskers can toast your bread, bagels, or English muffins, reheat your leftovers, and even bake small items. They heat up faster than conventional ovens and use less energy.

COFFEE MAKER. If you're a coffee drinker and you don't want to live on instant grounds stirred into boiling water, you need some way to brew yourself a cup or two in the morning. Whether you need a bells-and-whistles appliance that also shoots out cappuccino and espresso is up to you.

MICROWAVE. We'll admit the controversy right up front. Some people call them miracle machines and can't live without them. Others find them completely unnecessary. If you demand easy, fast ways to thaw frozen leftovers, reheat your coffee, pop popcorn, melt butter, and cook veggies while leaving most of their nutrients intact, you'll likely get your money's worth out of a small microwave.

utensils, etc.

KNIVES. Do not make do with the el cheapo knives hanging next to the rubber spatulas in the supermarket; they'll be dull in no time, making all your cutting and chopping a dreaded chore. Save up and invest in a good chopping knife, paring knife, and serrated knife at a department store. Treat them with care, and they'll last you a long time.

SPOONS. A slotted spoon, a ladle, and a large wooden spoon will cover all your basic mixing and scooping needs.

SPATULA. You can choose from either plastic or metal. If you have a teflon skillet, go with plastic. Metal will scrape off the coating, creating tiny flecks of teflon that will float around in your food.

GOOD-QUALITY CAN OPENER. Get one that's equipped with a bottle opener and a corkscrew.

VEGETABLE PEELER. A good one (we recommend a rubber-grip handle) makes it a piece of cake to peel apples for a pie or potatoes for a soup, shave carrot curls into a salad, or carry out other related tasks.

KITCHEN SCISSORS. This inexpensive utensil can make your life so much easier. Without searching for the other scissors you think you left somewhere near last winter's wrapping paper—wherever that is—you can cut open packages of pasta and snip sundried tomatoes into slivers.

DISH DRAINER. Drainers come in all styles, from wooden drying racks to tilted plastic contraptions that guide the drained water right into your sink.

COTTON DISHTOWELS. Buy a stack so you can replace dirty ones frequently. Bonus: dishtowels are a great way to play up (or provide) an accent color in your kitchen.

POT HOLDERS. Don't ruin your dishtowels by using them instead. Go ahead and spring for some flat holders, oven mitts, or both.

CLEANING TOOLS. You'll need a scouring pad and sponge near the sink, and perhaps a rag underneath it for mopping up spills.

SALT AND PEPPER SHAKERS. If it's an extra-long way from stove to table, buy one inexpensive plastic set with handles to use for cooking and another set to keep on the table.

dishes

True, dishes come in all sorts of appealing styles, from fine china to rustic stoneware. But if you've got a finite amount of space in your kitchen and limits to your tableware budget, your best bet is to put together a basic, neutral collection that'll look presentable all by itself and also provide a good backdrop for livelier accent pieces when you add them later.

Piece together a set of basic white or off-white dinner plates, smaller plates that can serve salad or dessert, and soup bowls. Eight of each piece should be plenty to start with, unless you're prone to huge dinner parties or absolutely never do dishes. Not all the pieces have to be the same style; just match the shades of white as closely as possible. You can find plain white dinnerware at kitchen-supply stores, department stores, discount retailers, even thrift stores. It often ranks among the least expensive. Search for simple, classic designs; avoid unusual or trendy looks. You're after a versatile set that will last.

Once you have a white foundation, you can begin to play with color and pattern. Sprinkle in a few pieces of your grandmother's pink Depression glass for a Valentine's dinner, or go ahead and splurge on those small black sushi plates you've been eyeing. Without owning a complete set of anything else, you'll still be able to easily change the mood and style of your table settings.

flatware

It was those pesky Victorians, the same people who gave us frilly trim on houses and books of manners, who came up with the concept of using a different utensil for every single eating activity (think aspic knives, pickle forks, and individual asparagus tongs). Fortunately, the rules have relaxed since the early 1900s. Today, you can get by just fine with nothing more than forks, knives, and spoons—eight of each. If you're feeling expansive, buy smaller salad forks and dessert spoons, too.

You want an all-purpose set of flatware that will go with anything, so stay away from colored handles, gold plating, and unusual designs for your basic pieces. Simple, silver-colored utensils are the most versatile. To get that silver color, you've got several choices: sterling silver, silver-plated flatware, and stainless steel. The first two are more expensive and require polishing (just how you want to spend a free Saturday, right?). Stainless is the way to go. It's affordable, nearly effortless to care for, and comes in styles ranging from sleek and modern to whimsical.

Avoid cheap flatware with thin handles. The poor-quality stuff has little chance of surviving that inevitable encounter with the garbage disposal—not to mention the other pressures of everyday life. Department stores and kitchenware stores typically carry several lines of good-quality flatware.

glassware

As with standard white dishes, plain clear glasses are best if you want a versatile collection of basics. Go ahead and part with the jumbo-sized plastic logo cups you collected over several spring break trips, and buy yourself a set of eight straight-sided tumblers instead. While you're at it, pick up eight short juice glasses, which can double as European-style wine glasses until you're able to invest in stemware.

The same department stores and kitchen stores that sell dishes and flatware carry affordable sets of glasses by the box. With your foundation in place, it's easy to mix in a variety of mismatched pieces, including glasses of different heights, colors, and styles, from antique cut glass to bright painted goblets.

bed

If you're like most people, you spend at least one-third of your life snoozing away in bed. In addition to something comfortable to sleep upon, you need a few other essential items to ensure that the time is well spent.

MATTRESS PAD. Fitted at its corners with elastic, this foundation piece provides a layer between the bottom sheet and the actual mattress. When your bed needs freshening, it's easy to whip off and toss in the wash. Buy one sized to fit your mattress.

SHEETS. Who knows why some people have entire linen closets full of sheets. If you've got two sets, you're covered—one set on the bed, one either camped in your laundry basket or clean and ready to offer to an out-of-town friend who's claimed your couch. Sheets typically come in sets: one fitted sheet, which snugs right over the mattress pad, and one flat sheet, to go on top of it. Cotton-blend sheets are the most affordable and easiest to care for (out of the wash and onto the bed). You might also consider a set of flannel sheets for winter if you live in a chilly climate. And unless you're absolutely sure you're going to like orange and blue polka dots as much a year from now as you do today, buy sheets in solid, neutral colors or with subtle, classic patterns.

PILLOWS. The range of pillow sizes includes everything from "boudoir" to "king." Though covering your bed with piles of different pillows is an easy way to give it some style, all you really need are a couple of standard-size pillows to prop you up while you read or cushion your head as you sleep.

PILLOW COVERS. Zippered pillow protectors serve the same purpose as a mattress pad—you can remove them and wash them regularly. On top of the protectors, you'll want pillowcases, which typically come in packages of two. Be sure to buy cases that are the same size as your pillows.

BLANKETS AND THE REST. Depending on the weather where you live (and sleep), you'll want either a cotton blanket, a wool blanket, or one of each, so you can switch with the seasons. What you add to the bed beyond that—bed skirt, pillow shams, bedspread, quilt, comforter, or throw—is primarily decor. In other words, if you have to, you can put those purchases off awhile.

bath

Each year, people spend an astounding amount of money on bath paraphernalia, from exotic salts, beads, oils, and soaps to imported sponges and scrubbers. The truth, of course, is that you can get squeaky clean with only a few affordable essential tools.

BATH TOWELS. In 1900, an American towel company invented a thick, pile fabric with loops on both sides. They called it terry cloth, and people around the world have been using the absorbent material to dry their bathed bodies since. Choose your terry-cloth towels in a size that suits your body (you can even find them in extra long, if that's what you need). Solid colors are best for mixing and matching with the other elements of your bathroom, with neutrals, once again, being the most versatile. (Buy purple towels decorated with pink fish, and you have to find a shower curtain and bath mat that don't clash—plus, you're definitely stuck with a theme.) If you hang your towel up to dry right after you use it, then reuse it for a week or so, two to four towels is plenty to have on hand. If you wad it up into a wet pile on the floor after each use, shame on you; you'll need to buy a dozen.

HAND TOWELS. Buy a color and style that match or complement your bath towels. Assuming you wash your hands before wiping them, two to four hand towels is all you need.

WASHCLOTHS. Same story as hand towels. Buy them to match or complement (or buy your towels and washcloths as a set); two to four is plenty.

SHOWER CURTAIN. Unless your bathroom has a shower stall with a door or a tub only, you can't live without a shower curtain. A plain liner-type curtain is all you really have to have to keep water from spraying the room. Add the decorative outer curtain if you want one later.

BATH MAT. Who wants to step out of the shower or tub on a winter morning (or anytime) and feel a cold, slippery floor beneath their feet? Make your bathroom cozy and keep the floor dry with a small mat.

keeping clean

Not long after you take up residence in your apartment, you'll start to notice that you now not only have your very own place, but also your very own dust bunnies, toothpaste splatters, and intermittent colonies of mildew and mold. This is not because you're doing something wrong. Your living spaces have always collected debris. If you're lucky, you've simply had someone else keeping it under control for you until now.

Let go of the fact that you never imagined yourself boning up on grease removal and toilet cleaners. These basic tips and easy tricks for keeping your apartment livable and presentable aren't meant to take over your life, merely to help you make sure a relatively clear path runs through it.

THE NITTY-GRITTY ON DIRT

Every surface collects dust and other deposits, from pet hair and food residue to grit from the outside world. We typically lump it all into the general category of dirt. Places where you regularly put your hands are especially susceptible. Look around the room right now, and you can probably spot signs of use on doors, door frames, light switches, and handles. Other places are less prone to hand smudges but perfect targets for dusty buildup: furniture surfaces, baseboards, the tops of door frames and windows.

SURFACE DIRT that's left alone long enough congeals into nasty grime. (Who likes to be ignored?) Giving all your surfaces a clean wipe regularly, before they have a chance to reach the grimy stage, is one of the most efficient uses of your limited housecleaning time. A good old-fashioned dust rag will do in lots of cases. To remove stickier stuff, maybe on countertops or the refrigerator door, use a squirt of one of the all-purpose cleaning solutions listed on page 51.

FLOORS also provide dust and dirt with one big, convenient surface on which to collect, making regular vacuuming or sweeping and mopping another efficient way to head off major buildup. When you're really going all out, move the furniture and hit those hidden spots that are likely harboring a few crumbs and cobwebs of their own. Take area rugs outside and give them a good shake.

KITCHENS benefit from a little additional scrubbing. Not only does the stove top need to be cleaned (much easier, by the way, if you wipe it down each time you use it rather than every six months), but you'll also want to clean up splattered grease and food off the walls around the stove. If your stove top doesn't have a hood or vent, you should probably run a damp cloth over whatever's directly above the stove, too. The kitchen sink, home on any given day to vegetable peels, food-caked plates, and used coffee filters, will be a much happier place to look at if it's the recipient of a thorough scrubbing every so often. And while you're at it, give the cabinet doors and the surfaces of all your appliances a swipe with a detergent-soaked cloth or sponge. The inside of the refrigerator is a whole other story. Read on.

BATHROOMS are a lot like kitchens. They get super-frequent use, so they need slightly more concentrated cleaning. Bathtubs host soap scum (and mildew, if you wait long enough between cleanings). Sinks can become caked with toothpaste spittle and congested with hair in no time. Toilets—well, we all know what goes in there. Put on some rubber gloves, prepare the cleaning solutions on page 51, grab a sponge and a toilet brush, and have at it every week or so.

cleaning the fridge

If you've recently noticed an odor that surfaces every time you open your refrigerator door—one that's the opposite of appetizing—or if you've become aware of bergs in your freezer that could scuttle the Titanic, it's time to tend to the appliance you depend on to keep your food cool and fresh.

BASIC CLEANING

Unplug the refrigerator and remove everything in it. Pull out the removable parts (shelves and such), and wash them with a mild detergent in warm water. Rinse and dry them. Wash the interior walls and door with 1 to 2 tablespoons (7 to 14 g) of baking soda mixed into one quart (.95 L) warm water. Wipe the surfaces dry and leave the door open to air out the inside. Don't use commercial cleansers, chlorine bleach, or cleaning waxes on refrigerators; they can damage or corrode the plastics.

Maybe you're performing these activities not as a part of basic (that is, regular) cleaning, but as an intervention measure. In that case, the situation might call for a few more steps. If you've removed the months-old carry-out containers and washed the inside of the refrigerator and it still stinks, spread baking soda in shallow dishes and put them on the shelves. Leave the refrigerator open and unplugged for a few hours, and the baking soda should absorb any residual odors. If it doesn't, replace it with kitty litter, imitation vanilla extract, or fresh ground coffee, close the door, and run the refrigerator empty for several days.

DEFROSTING

If you don't have the self-defrosting type, you should defrost the freezer about once a year, unless frost builds up to more than $1/2$ inch (1.3 cm) thick before then. Unplug the refrigerator, put on kitchen gloves to protect your hands from freezer burn, and scrape the frost out of the freezer, using a wooden or plastic scraper. Collect the ice chunks in a plastic bowl, tossing them in the sink when the bowl is full. Never use a sharp instrument to scrape with—the freezer coils are easy to damage, and so's your flesh. After you've cleared out all the frost, clean the freezer using the same system described for the inside of the refrigerator.

caring for carpets

If your apartment has wall-to-wall carpeting, you're going to need a vacuum cleaner. Only a few sections of the plush stuff? Then some serious sweeping might suffice. Regardless of the amount of carpet you're dealing with, use the following tips to keep it in shape.

■ To prevent excessive wear, note your frequent routes. Buy cheap, sturdy rugs to place over the carpet in high-traffic areas.

■ If you spill something, deal with it then. Carpets are usually treated with stain-resistant chemicals, so if you act quickly, you should be able to keep it from staining. First, blot the area until it's completely dry with a clean, dry cloth or a paper towel; scrubbing will only spread the stain. As you blot, work from the edge of the spill inward, again, to prevent spreading. If your spill is semi-solid, scrape it gently with a metal spoon after you blot it. Vacuum the area after you scrape as much of the spill off as you can. Next, clean the area with the detergent solution on page 51, or see the tips to the right on removing specific stains. If you decide to use a chemical spot remover, test it on a hidden area beforehand to make sure it won't damage the carpet.

■ Unless you signed a contract requiring you to steam-clean or provide other special cleaning of your carpeting before moving out, don't bother. Consumer studies show that results vary widely, and the service is costly.

REMOVING COMMON STAINS FROM CARPET AND FABRIC

You can either make your apartment off limits to everyone else in the world, then stand completely still in the center of a room while you're there alone, or you can go ahead and live life and use these remedies to deal with any fallout.

WINE OR GRAPE JUICE

Blot up as much of the spill as possible, then neutralize the area with a white vinegar solution: $\frac{1}{3}$ cup (90 mL) of white vinegar mixed with $\frac{2}{3}$ cup (160 mL) of water. Use the detergent solution on page 51 to remove the stain.

BLOOD

Everything you use on a blood stain must be cool. Heat will set the stain and make it permanent. Blot up as much of the blood as possible, then neutralize it by saturating the spot with an ammonia solution (see page 51). Continue to blot the stain. If this doesn't remove all the blood, try using the detergent solution on page 51—but remember to make it with cold water.

OIL

Oil and water don't mix—that's why it's so hard to clean oil out of anything. Your best bet is to apply isopropyl rubbing alcohol to a clean cloth, paper towel, or cotton ball, and dab the oil spot until it disappears. If this doesn't work, use a detergent solution (see page 51).

RUST

Rust can often form where the metal legs of a piece of furniture rub against the carpet. To remove the rust stains, spray lemon juice on the spot. Saturate it completely, and wait five minutes. Then blot up as much of the lemon juice as possible with a paper towel. Clean the lemon juice out of the carpet using the detergent solution on page 51.

BUBBLE GUM

Rub an ice cube over the gum to freeze it, then shatter the gum and vacuum it up.

WAX

Spread a brown paper bag over the hardened wax, and iron the bag with a warm iron. The paper will absorb the wax.

LAST-DITCH STAIN REMOVAL

If none of these solutions remove the stain, try moistening the area with three-percent hydrogen peroxide. Let it sit for an hour, then blot the stain. Repeat until the stain is gone. You won't need to rinse this solution—sunlight turns hydrogen peroxide into water.

a sensitive subject: you and your toilet

Commode. John. Porcelain God. As with many objects that are important but intimate, we use nicknames for the appliance that services us behind closed doors. But regardless of what you call it, if you don't provide your toilet with a regular dose of basic maintenance, it's not going to keep it a secret (toilets, don't forget, are frequently used by guests). Also, toilets use more water than any other appliance—up to 40 percent of your apartment's total water consumption. If your toilet isn't working properly, you could be flushing a lot of money away.

CAN YOU HEAR IT?

Most of the time, fixing a running toilet or one that doesn't flush properly is pretty simple. The first step is to take the cover off of the tank. At the bottom of the tank (all the water in there is clean!) there's a rubber flapper with a chain attached to it. If this chain is too loose, the rubber flapper could get caught between the flange and the gasket, meaning it won't seal the drain and the toilet will "run" or drain constantly. To fix this, shorten the chain by removing a few links with needle-nose pliers. Likewise, if the chain is twisted or kinked up, making it too short and tight, it'll hold up the gasket and let water seep through. Just untangle it.

If the chain isn't the problem, your toilet could be malfunctioning because the water level in the tank is too high or too low. To the right of the handle (again, on the inside of the tank) is an open tube called the overflow pipe. The water level should be ½ inch (1.3 cm) below this opening. If it isn't, you'll need to adjust the floatball (the thing that looks like a rubber balloon). To raise the water level, bend the arm that is attached to the float ball up. To lower the water level, bend the float arm down.

If neither of these things works, make sure there is no buildup on the rubber stopper or the seat that it fits on. Gently scour both the rim of the stopper and the seat so that the stopper will fit snugly. If that doesn't fix your toilet problems, call your landlord.

IT WON'T FLUSH, OR WORSE

If your toilet clogs, get a toilet plunger and put some petroleum jelly on the rim of the cup. Place the plunger over the hole at the bottom of the toilet bowl at an angle. (This will keep air from getting trapped under the cup.) There should be enough water in the bowl to cover the plunger cup. Hold the plunger upright, and push it up and down several times. This should "burp" the clog through and fix your problem. When you finish, rinse your used plunger in a mixture of one part bleach to 10 parts water.

LEAKS, PUDDLES, AND THE LIKE

If the toilet is leaking water onto the floor, it has probably shifted on its base. When a toilet shifts, the wax seal that keeps the water in breaks. To fix this, simply sit on the toilet and twist it back into its proper place. If this doesn't stop the leak, call your landlord.

In the case of absolute toilet chaos, turn off the water supply to the toilet. The shut-off valve is on a silver pipe that goes into the tank (usually on the left). Turn the handle clockwise to turn the water off, then get help from your landlord.

elementary drain theory

The drain is where the water goes after it flows out of the faucet and takes a spin around the sink or tub. That's the idea, anyway. But if food, hair, and other objects have also been filling the drain over time, it will reach a point where it no longer does what its name suggests.

PREVENTIVE MEASURES ARE THE BEST WAY TO AVOID CLOGGED DRAINS.

■ If you don't have a garbage disposal, don't pretend you do. Scrape all food scraps into the trash or compost bin before rinsing dishes. Piling food-laden plates in the sink is only inviting trouble.

■ Don't trim your bangs or shave over the bathroom sink, then rinse all the clippings down. Clean them out with a damp paper towel, and toss them in the trash.

■ Once a month, pour a few gallons of boiling water down each of your drains. The boiling water will dissolve buildup in the pipes.

Once a clog has formed, the best way to unclog it is mechanically (i.e., with elbow grease) rather than chemically. Most chemical treatments can handle minor clogs, but are not very effective otherwise. The more caustic chemicals are also hazardous to use and can even damage the pipes. Instead, try the drain cleaner solution on page 51 first. If the baking soda doesn't clear out the clog, get your plunger and some gloves. Stick the plunger cup to the area over the drain, and fill the sink with enough water to cover the cup. If you have a double sink or an overflow opening, block the second opening with a wet rag. Plunge up and down until the clog comes loose, then discard the debris. Pour boiling water down the drain to flush out any remaining debris.

If the clog in your drain persists despite your efforts, call your landlord. Some of the plumbing may have to be taken apart to find and fix the problem.

bugging out

The best way to keep unwanted guests away, you may have already discovered, is to refrain from supplying them with free meals. In the case of bugs, always store your food (especially sugar and flour) in airtight containers. Clean your counters, tables, and stove top immediately after cooking and eating. If you're going to leave the dishes until the next morning, at least scrape and rinse them.

If you end up hosting insect pests anyway, here are some deterrents, followed by a few "Fatal Final Measures"—for bugs who can't take a hint.

ANTS. Follow the trail and block their entrance with a dab of caulk. If you don't have any handy, squeeze lemon juice into the crack, then cut up the lemon and put it around the entrance. Wash surface areas with equal parts vinegar and water. **FATAL FINAL MEASURE:** *Mix 1 cup (140g) of flour with 2 cups (280g) of borax (which you can typically find at hardware stores or sometimes with laundry soap in the grocery store), and sprinkle the mixture around the foundation of your building (if you're on the ground floor) or around the ants' entrance. (Borax is highly toxic; make sure no child or pet eats it.)*

FLIES. Cover your garbage tightly. When you take out the trash, wash the garbage can thoroughly with soap and water. After it dries, sprinkle dry soap or borax into the can. **FATAL FINAL MEASURE:** *Make your own fly paper. Bring equal parts of sugar, corn syrup, and water to a boil, then spread the mixture onto brown paper, and hang it near problem areas. Avoid walking into it, and change it frequently.*

ROACHES. Never leave food out—not even pet food! Since roaches don't have many friends, all the suggestions we have are **FATAL FINAL MEASURES:** ❶ *If you don't have to worry about children or pets eating toxic substances, mix 2 tablespoons (14g) of flour with 4 tablespoons (28g) of borax and 1 tablespoon (7g) of cocoa. Put the mixture into shallow dishes, and leave it out for a roach's* **Last Supper.** *If you think this would be a terrible abuse of chocolate, mix ½ cup (98g) of borax with ¼ cup (35g) of flour, and sprinkle the powder along baseboards and door sills.* ❷ *If you need a child- or pet-safe solution, mix equal parts of baking soda and powdered sugar. Spread the mixture around the infested area. It will kill the roaches, but only taste terrible to other creatures.*

the only five cleaning products you'll ever need

Perusing aisles and aisles of cleaning products can leave you in a fresh-scented daze. Take heart—there are only five things you'll need to clean anything in your apartment, and you can buy all of them in one quick visit to a grocery store.

1 White distilled vinegar is used in many common cleaning solutions.

2 Dish soap or detergent is another common cleaning substance. Brands that are dye- and fragrance-free and don't contain lanolin or bleach are best for mixing with other products to create other cleaning solutions (read on).

3 Ammonia is also commonly used in cleaning solutions.

4 Baking soda neutralizes acidic odors and is slightly abrasive.

5 Washing soda is stronger than baking soda. You'll find it in the store's laundry section. Always wear gloves when using washing soda.

basic cleaning solutions using your five products

DETERGENT SOLUTION (ALL-PURPOSE)
Mix ¼ teaspoon (1.25 mL) of liquid dishwashing detergent with 1 cup (240 mL) of lukewarm water.

**AMMONIA SOLUTION
(ALL-PURPOSE; ESPECIALLY GOOD FOR KITCHENS AND BATHS)**
Mix 2 tablespoons (15 mL) of household ammonia per cup (240 mL) of water.

**WASHING SODA SOLUTION
(ALL-PURPOSE; GREAT FOR SERIOUS GRIME AND MILDEW)**
Mix ½ teaspoon (2.5 mL) of washing soda with 2 cups (480 mL) of hot water in a spray bottle.

WINDOW CLEANER
Pour ¼ cup (60 mL) of white vinegar, 2 cups (480 mL) of water and ½ teaspoon (2.5 mL) of liquid detergent into a spray bottle.

FURNITURE CLEANER
Combine ¼ cup (60 mL) of white vinegar in a bowl with a few drops of vegetable oil.

SCOURING POWDER
You can use straight baking soda for this.

SOFT SCRUBBER
Mix ¼ cup (35 g) of baking soda with enough liquid detergent to create a frosting-like consistency.

DRAIN CLEANER
Pour 1 cup (140 g) of baking soda down the drain, followed by 3 cups (720 mL) of boiling water.

OVEN CLEANER
Sprinkle ¼ inch (6 mm) of baking soda over the bottom of the oven. Keep the baking soda moist by periodically spraying water on it. Let it sit for six hours or overnight, then scoop the baking soda out and rinse the oven well.

**Always rinse all these solutions thoroughly.
Any residue will attract dirt quickly.**

PROJECTS & IDEAS

We start with your apartment's surface elements: walls, floors, and windows. If you're the only first-apartment dweller in the whole world who's entirely satisfied with these features just the way they are, skip ahead. If not, sift through our plans for doctoring, decorating, and, when necessary, disguising them. After that, we move on to ways you can use lighting, furniture, accessories, and storage tactics to turn your apartment's bare rooms into a home that's undeniably your own.

walls

You can't miss them, so it's best if you enjoy looking at them. We give you ways to both play up your walls and to cover them over, depending on what you have to work with.

paint just one

Dark to airy, or sterile to cozy. The section on wall-painting basics, page 22, tells you how to successfully coat the walls of your apartment with fresh paint. Here are some of the reasons (besides the fact that it's faster and easier) that you might want to stop at one.

DEFINITION. If a room is especially boxy, meaning it's in danger of looking boring, painting one wall a color that's different from the rest is a good way to give it some dimension. It's also an easy way to accent the interesting lines of a room that's anything but boxy, such as the bedroom of the converted attic apartment shown here.

DRAMA. Paint all four walls citron green or the deep red of your velvet love seat, and chances are it'll be too much. But cover just one wall in a brave new color, and you have a definite statement.

SEPARATION. Maybe one section of your small space serves as your home office. Or, perhaps your sleeping and living areas must coexist within the same four walls. Painting one of those walls a different color can help visually separate one area from another.

COHERENCE. At the same time wall colors can help separate the contents of a room, they can also tie them together. Say the only link among your otherwise motley collection of furniture and accessories is the saffron stripe on the sofa that matches the lamp shade on the other side of the room. Splash that same saffron on the wall between the two, and you have instant unity.

clip cord

You have neither the time nor the energy to purchase and mount one of those boring cork-and-wood bulletin boards so you can pin up all your postcards, concert tickets, and bills. Nevertheless, the wall in front of your work space is the perfect holding place for odds and ends like these. Here's the simple—dare we say idiot-proof?—and elegant way out. Tack up one or more clip cords as you need them.

WHAT YOU NEED

Push pins, decorative tacks, screw eyes, screw hooks, or nails

A not-too-stretchy cord: cotton string, nylon cord, picture wire, plastic coated electrical or cable wire are all options

Colored paper clips, bulldog clips, clothespins, decorative bobby pins, etc.

WHAT YOU DO

1 Cut a length of your cord. Three or four feet (90 to 120 cm) will suffice. Too long a cord will droop.

2 Based on your wall (and the terms of your lease), determine what type of anchors you'll use to hang your cord. A temporary, movable, and low-impact choice would be pushpins or tacks. More permanent anchors—nails and screw eyes—will leave larger holes to fill if you move them or leave the apartment.

3 Hang your light bill and the postcards from Cancun from the cord with simple clips. Use only one type of clip on the cord to unify the display; mix clips if you want it more vibrant. Change the display frequently. If you don't pay the light bill on time, display the cut-off notice as a piece of whimsy.

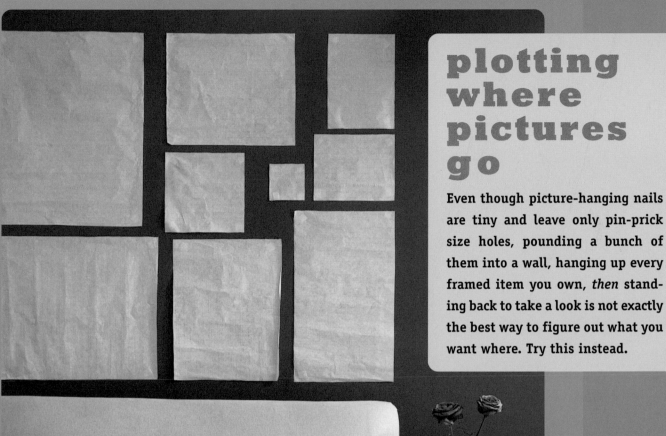

plotting where pictures go

Even though picture-hanging nails are tiny and leave only pin-prick size holes, pounding a bunch of them into a wall, hanging up every framed item you own, *then* standing back to take a look is not exactly the best way to figure out what you want where. Try this instead.

PICTURE THIS

You don't have to own paintings or photographs to cover your walls with interesting colors, lines, and shapes. Wall art comes in all kinds of forms. Try framing and hanging:

Postcards

Maps

Fabric remnants

Vintage game boards

Typed poems

Old letters

Pressed flowers and leaves

Playing cards

Steamed-off labels from bottles of wine or imported olive oil

Blueprints

Old album covers

Pages from a 1950s cookbook, etiquette book, or cocktail-making guide

In case you somehow missed this little gem of information back when you were living in a college dorm, here's one of life's timeless tips: to fill nail holes in a wall, use plain white toothpaste. It won't sink into the holes the way spackling compound often does.

WHAT YOU DO

1 Trace all your pictures onto pieces of paper (paper bags work well), and cut out the shapes.

2 If the backs of the framed pictures are equipped with hanging wire, pull the wire taut on each, and measure from the top of the wire's arc to the top of the frame. On the matching paper template, measure down from the top edge the distance of your measurement, and mark where the picture-hanging nail or hook will meet the wire. If the backs of your pictures feature saw-toothed hangers rather than wire, measure how far down they are from the top edge on each picture, and transfer those marks to the corresponding templates.

3 Use a low-tack tape (both drafting tape and painter's tape work well) to hang the templates on the wall (marked sides facing out), then reconfigure them as much as you like, until you're happy with where each is hanging.

4 Hammer your nails (and picture hooks, if you're using them) through the marks on the templates and right into the wall, then rip the paper off and hang your pictures.

CONFIGURATIONS

STAIR STEPPING. Align the center points of your pictures diagonally.

TOPS OR BOTTOMS IN ALIGNMENT. Draw together a group of various-sized pictures by aligning all their tops or all their bottoms along an imaginary horizontal line.

COMBINATION ALIGNMENT. Divide a larger group of various-sized pictures into two or more rows, and align the tops of the top-row pictures and the bottoms of the bottom-row pictures on imaginary horizontal lines, then line up the sides as well. The grouping on the preceding page is an example of combination alignment.

GALLERY STYLE. Hang identical-sized pictures in a long, neat row, either horizontal or vertical.

MOSAIC. Anything goes, with a bit of method to the madness. Give your mosaic display some balance by aligning the bottoms of some frames with the tops of others and/or by centering some pictures over others. You can also soften a rigid-looking arrangement by adding in a few rounded or octagonal frames.

problem

You've just signed a lease with the world's strictest landlord. No painting, no mounting a spice rack in the kitchen, no hanging pictures on any wall anywhere. The upside is, the apartment is in fabulous shape—no previous tenant has been allowed to alter any of its surfaces either. The trouble, of course, is that those pristine walls are awfully bare.

fix

Fortunately, there's a simple solution that makes those bare walls look as if they belong in a trendy gallery: artfully prop pictures, paintings, mirrors, and other framed pieces right up against them. Rest large pieces like this full-length mirror on the floor. Ledges, molding strips, mantles, and the tops of freestanding shelf units, benches, and tables all work well as bases for smaller ones.

five-step plan for finding the right roommate

So, your budget dictates the need for a roommate. Thrilled? Terrified? Relax and follow these five steps.

1. Clarify for Yourself What You Expect

A roommate is a person who shares expenses and space; a roommate is not a guaranteed best friend. However, a roommate must be someone you can trust to respect you, your privacy, and your belongings. Articulate what that means for you. Would you rather your new roommate not have lots of out-of-town visitors who stay with you? Do you expect that you and your roommate will have separate phone lines? What amount of noise is acceptable? At what hour should acceptable noise end so that either roommate can enjoy the silence and work, study, or sleep? Are smoking and drinking acceptable? When and where?

2. Meet the Would-Be Roommates

Depending on your community and situation, you may run an ad, post a flyer, or use word-of-mouth to come up with a pool of potential roommates. Meet with each, ideally in a public place. Share the list of expectations you came up with in step 1. Let her or him know the facts of your lifestyle and the living situation you want, then move on to the discussion items in step 3. If you're interviewing several people, make notes so you remember who said what. If you sense that someone would be a good roommate, collect contact information for references.

3. Five Topics You Must Discuss

These issues come up constantly, regardless of the age or lifestyle of roommates. Talk about them now.

BILL PAYING

You want all bills divided equally and paid on time. Discuss who will make payments and in whose name the lease and utilities will be. (It's best to list all roommates.) Agree that nonessential services (cable television, cable modem, magazine subscriptions) must be negotiated beforehand or will be paid for by the roommate who orders them.

GUESTS

Guests can feel like invaders if you haven't adopted rules to govern their behavior. Agree on the answers to the questions of who, what, when, where, how long, and overnight or not. Also, "house rules" about pets, smoking or drinking, borrowing, and privacy should apply to guests as well.

CLEANLINESS

What's "clean enough"? Who will clean what, and how often? You want chores shared, guaranteeing clean shared rooms (bathroom, kitchen, living room).

PERSONAL POSSESSIONS

If you want to avoid hassles about who ate the last piece of cake and used up the shampoo, agree from the start not to share anything but toilet paper.

SAFETY

Should doors and windows be locked when you're home, when you're sleeping, and/or when no one is home? Where will an extra key be kept? Who else gets a key?

4. Check References

Talk to former roommates, landlords, and the current employer of your would-be roommates. Ask about their bill-paying history. Verify a steady income. Check out any concerns you have.

5. Make the Decision

You've spoken with many interesting people you might never have otherwise met. You've been charmed and repelled. You've checked out their stories. You should be as ready as you'll ever be now to decide whose personality and lifestyle is most compatible with yours.

www.larkbooks.com

@ Café
9:45

cover-up message center

If you've got an ugly or even just a blank wall you'd rather not have staring you in the face, here's a useful way to cover a huge portion of it. Frame up a panel of white board next to a panel of steel (you can buy these as big as you like), and you've got one spot for jotting erasable notes and another for sticking lists, both conveniently located right next to each other. Bonus: it's a cinch to make your message center completely your own with a set of personalized magnets.

WHAT YOU NEED

Piece of ½-inch (1.3cm) plywood for the base (This one measures 28 x 34 inches [71.1 x 86.4cm].)

Panel of 26-gauge steel and one of white tile board (These pieces need to cover the unframed portion of your plywood base, with the tile board overlapping the steel by about ½ inch [1.3cm]. The steel here measures 16 x 26 inches [40.6 x 66 cm], and the tile board measures 15 x 24 inches [38.1 x 61 cm].)

2¼-inch (5.7cm) primed molding (You need two pieces to frame the long sides of your message center and two pieces to frame the short sides.)

Liquid nails (the kind in a tube)

Black spray paint

Acrylic paints

Finishing nails

Wood filler

Picture-hanging kit (screw eyelets, wire, etc.)

Handsaw

Miter box (This inexpensive contraption serves as a guide for your saw when you make angled cuts.)

Small artist's brushes

Hammer

WHAT YOU DO

1 The home improvement store where you buy your supplies should be able to cut almost everything to size for you. All you'll have to do is make the 45° diagonal cuts where the molding fits together—known as miter cuts. The miter box will guide your saw so you can cut the ends of your molding pieces (see figure 1).

2 Place the tile board and steel on top of the plywood base. Put the tile board on the left and the steel on the right, with the tile board overlapping the steel by ½ inch (1.3cm). Place the molding around the edges, making sure everything fits before you glue it all together.

3 Remove the molding, and trace the outside edges of the tile board and steel, so you have a guide for putting them back in place.

4 Remove the tile board and steel, coat the back of each panel with liquid nails, and set them back in place. Liquid nails work best if you run a bead of the adhesive about ½ inch (1.3cm) in from the edge of each panel, then drizzle it all over the center. Clean up any misplaced adhesive with hot soapy water right away.

5 Place books or other heavy objects on the corners of the glued panels and down the center where they overlap, and let them dry.

6 Spray the molding black and let it dry. If you like, add detail lines or dots around the molding in other paint colors. The bottom end of an artist's brush is perfect for dabbing on paint dots.

7 Glue the molding around the edges of the message center with liquid nails; it'll overlap both the tile board and the steel slightly.

8 Once the adhesive on the molding is dry, use finishing nails around the edges to further secure it to the plywood.

9 If necessary, use wood filler to spackle any variations in the molding where you pounded the nails or around the corners, then touch up the areas with paint.

10 Install screw eyelets on the back, following the directions on the picture-hanging kit.

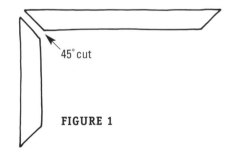

45° cut

FIGURE 1

making magnets

Home improvement stores sell small sets of magnets (rounds, squares, rectangles, etc.), as well as magnetic paper with an adhesive front. To turn these raw materials into one-of-a-kind magnets for the steel side of your message center, either hot glue trinkets (shellacked and painted dog bones, for example) to the magnets, or attach photos to the adhesive side of the magnetic paper, and cut them out.

spiffing up by season

Flip to the opening calendar spread of a certain home decorating magazine (we're not naming names), and, depending on the time of year, you'll be told that October 6 is the day for piling red apples in a wooden bowl or that, come the first Saturday in April, you'd better be coloring eggs. We're guessing that you may not be quite so exacting about plotting what you'll do when. Still, it's nice to do something to celebrate the natural wonder of moving from one season to another.

SPRING

Fasten a row of hand-made straw whisk brooms to your wall. (Great substitute for actual spring cleaning!)

Hand-stitch sheer pockets onto a light-weight curtain, and put pressed flowers (or four-leaf clovers if you can find them) inside.

Put window boxes on your windowsills, and fill them with potted pansies.

Force some bulbs, maybe paper whites or amaryllis.

Weave greenery or budding branches around a light fixture.

Remove the labels from metal cans, paint the cans with a creamy color, and use them as vases for the season's first flowers.

Find an umbrella printed with a motif you like (rubber ducks, multiple Mona Lisa faces, etc.), and place it, opened, in a corner. Skip this one if you're superstitious, of course.

SUMMER

Turn a light cotton tapestry into a no-sew slip-cover. Just throw it over a couch or chair, and tuck it in around the edges.

Put driftwood, water-smoothed rocks, and clear bottles filled with sand on display. If you like, drop decorative slips of paper in the bottles, telling where the sand came from or naming the friends or family you were with when you collected it.

Fill a clear pitcher with whole lemons.

String paper lanterns around a room.

Make a bouquet out of nothing but fresh herbs.

Burn candles inside glass lanterns or hurricanes.

Stick pictures from your favorite childhood summer vacations around the edges of a mirror—or upright in a bowl of beach sand.

Pile produce from a local outdoor market in a big bowl for an instant summery centerpiece.

Stack all your favorite summer reads beside a table lamp, then top off the stack with a seashell or two.

FALL

Switch some of your lightbulbs to rose or gold.

String colorful leaves into garlands to hang over doors or windows.

Fill a few interesting jars with nuts still in their shells, and stack them in a clever way on your coffee table.

Add a layer of uncooked wild rice or unpopped popcorn to the bottom of a tray, and nestle votive candles in it.

Use a shallow, open basket as a container for odd-shaped squashes and gourds (you can buy these by the sack at supermarkets).

Laminate some of the prettiest leaves outside your door (a print shop can do this), cut them out, and use them as coasters.

Arrange barley, wheat, or other dried grasses in tin flower buckets (craft stores sell them), or tie them up with raffia and hang them upside down from doorknobs or hooks in the wall.

WINTER

Drape a cozy blanket or shawl over the back of the couch.

Cut out paper snow-flakes, and dangle them at different heights by clear thread in your windows.

Dust pinecones, seed pods, and pomegranates lightly with glitter, and show them off in bowls or baskets.

Run a row of poinsettias along a hallway, windowsill, or wall.

Fill a colored-glass cup with a collection of thermometers (even better if some are from an antique shop).

Make a bouquet out of bare, twisted branches.

Create a bowl of good cheer by filling it with tiny, sparkly tree ornaments and a strand of minilights.

Push a bunch of red and white plastic tacks randomly into a wall, and hang candy canes from them.

hanging walls

We all know walls are a good thing to tear down when it comes to divided countries and blocked communication. But in a small, open apartment where you have a lot going on, you may wish you could put a few more up. Floor-to-ceiling sheetrock is probably not an option, but here are two simple fabric partitions that do a fine job of separating one area from another.

WHAT YOU DO

1 Iron your curtain panel.

2 Measure the width of the panel. Add 2 inches (5.1 cm) to the measurement, measure and mark the dowel with this longer measurement, and cut the dowel to size with the handsaw.

3 The lattice strip will weight the bottom of the panel, so it hangs straight and flat. To determine the length you need, slide the strip into the hem casing at the bottom of the panel. Push one end even with the edge of the panel, and mark the opposite end where the other edge of the panel hits. Remove the strip and use the handsaw to cut it just inside the mark.

4 The fabric panels in the apartment shown here hang from an exposed pipe that just happens to span the right portion of the room. If your apartment is missing this handy feature, you can hang your panels from ceiling hooks (the same sort used for hanging plant baskets). Attach the ceiling hooks to the ceiling, spacing them so they'll be a couple of inches (5.1 cm) in from the ends of the dowel rod.

5 Insert the dowel into the rod pocket. Clip each end of the dowel rod with the curtain ring clips, and hang the ring portions from the ceiling hooks.

6 Insert the lattice strip in the bottom hem casing.

hanging walls variation ONE

WHAT YOU NEED

Curtain panels with rod pockets

Wooden dowel (Be sure the diameter fits the rod pocket at the top of the curtain panel. Buy a dowel longer than your curtain panel is wide; you'll cut it to size.)

Wooden lattice strip (Again, buy a strip that's longer than you need so you can cut it to size.)

Wall or ceiling anchors with hooks

Curtain rings with clips

Iron

Measuring tool

Handsaw

Use copper plumbing pipe that's $1/2$ to $3/4$ inch thick (1.3 to 1.9 cm) in place of the wooden dowels and lattice strips, if you want panels with more of an industrial look. You can have your pipe cut at the home improvement store where you purchase it.

If you're on friendly terms with a sewing machine, you can sew your own panels from any fabric you like—or from plain muslin you've dressed up yourself with rubber stamps and fabric ink. Just stitch a simple casing at the top and bottom of the fabric for the dowel and lattice strip.

WHAT YOU DO

1 Measure the height and width of the space where you want your hanging wall. Purchase a pair (or more) of ready-made curtain panels to fit it. Count the number of tabs or ties on each curtain panel; you'll need at least that many pegs. The more pegs you have, the more flexibility you have when you're positioning the panels.

2 Purchase your board and pegs at a home improvement store. Most stores offer free cuts on the lumber you purchase. If you don't want to saw the board to size, have it done at the store.

3 Measure and mark your board at 6-inch (15.2 cm) intervals. Screw the pegs into the board at each mark. To make it easier, make starter holes for the pegs by driving a nail partway into the board at each mark or drilling partway in with a bit about the same size as the screw.

4 Cover your work area, and paint the board and pegs. (Anything goes here: board one color, pegs another; colors that match or contrast with the others in the room; up to you.) Let the paint dry, then recoat everything as needed.

5 Drill a hole at each end of the board with a bit approximately the same size as your drywall screw.

6 Get a friend to help you hold the board in place while you screw it into the wall at each end. Be sure you screw into a stud (a piece of the wooden frame behind the wall) each time. The studs should be right where you need them for a job like this; they're always on either side of windows and doorways.

7 Hang the curtains on the pegs.

hanging walls variation TWO

This variation also makes a good door if you're missing one in a crucial spot (entryway, closet opening, etc.). Or, it can be adapted to work as a window covering.

WHAT YOU NEED

Ready-made tab-top or tie-top curtain panels

Strip of board cut to match the width of the area you want to cover

Wooden pegs with screws

Acrylic or latex paint

Finish nails or drywall screws

Measuring tool

Handsaw (optional)

Drill and drill bits (optional)

Screwdriver

Paintbrush

Hammer

Stepladder or sturdy chair

A friend with nothing to do

home electronics

If recorded music, cable cooking shows, and Internet access seem as necessary to you as indoor plumbing, you're going to have to invest in some gadgetry. What you buy and where you put it will depend on a number of factors: lifestyle, budget, and apartment size—not to mention number of outlets and phone jacks. Here are a few tips for selecting and setting up home electronics.

first things first

Home electronics are generally expensive. Base your buys on what your lifestyle demands and allows. Don't own any compact discs or vinyl albums, and don't expect to anytime soon? Get a clock radio instead of a stereo. If you need to work your way up to a stereo, buy a small boom box that plays cassette tapes and CDs. Are movies at home one of your favorite escapes? Get a television and VCR or DVD player. Let your budget, apartment size, and personal priorities help you decide among a compact unit, an elaborate setup, or something in between. Do you do most of your Internet accessing from home rather than the office, or do you work from home? A hard drive, monitor, and Internet connection via your phone line are basics; a printer, scanner, CD burner, and cable modem are extras to consider, based on your situation.

location, location, location

Don't locate electronic equipment near water sources, such as kitchen faucets, leaky ceilings, or windows that are sometimes open. It's best to set up stereos, televisions, and the like against walls, so you and others will be less likely to bump and damage them. And, here's the big news flash: electronics require electricity. If you don't want cords running across floors or along long stretches of walls, place equipment near outlets. Avoid overloading your wiring, and notify your landlord if you have problems.

special care for specific equipment

STEREO. If you've invested in a full stereo system (receiver, amp, CD player, tape deck, record player, speakers), stack the components, following the manufacturer's recommendations. You may need a multi-outlet extension cord to plug in all the pieces. Place speakers at least 6 feet (1.8m) apart and at the same height, level with where your ears will be when listening. (Most likely, that's seated in a chair or couch 6 feet [1.8m] from and centered between the speakers.) Run speaker wires along wall bases or under rugs.

HOME ENTERTAINMENT CENTER. Store the elements of a home entertainment center (large television, VCR or DVD player, speakers, gaming equipment), in a prefabricated unit, on appropriate shelving, or on sturdy end tables. Again, you may need a multi-outlet extension cord to plug in all the pieces. Position at least some of the room's seating, centered on the television screen, 6 feet (1.8m) away. Lamplight causes less interference with television screens than overhead lighting.

COMPUTER. Treat yourself to some in-home ergonomics, including a desk that doesn't hold your computer so high you have to look up at it and a comfortable chair. Position your setup so your screen isn't hit with direct light from a window. Keep accessories (CD burner, scanner, printer, etc.) off the floor, preferably in a cart. One more time, you'll likely need that multi-outlet extension cord to connect all your pieces to your power source.

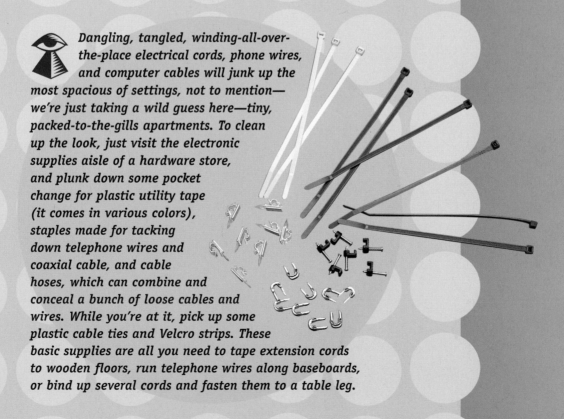

Dangling, tangled, winding-all-over-the-place electrical cords, phone wires, and computer cables will junk up the most spacious of settings, not to mention— we're just taking a wild guess here—tiny, packed-to-the-gills apartments. To clean up the look, just visit the electronic supplies aisle of a hardware store, and plunk down some pocket change for plastic utility tape (it comes in various colors), staples made for tacking down telephone wires and coaxial cable, and cable hoses, which can combine and conceal a bunch of loose cables and wires. While you're at it, pick up some plastic cable ties and Velcro strips. These basic supplies are all you need to tape extension cords to wooden floors, run telephone wires along baseboards, or bind up several cords and fasten them to a table leg.

wall cover two ways

In addition to glaring white, apartment walls can come in the following styles: cracked, scuffed, gouged, peeling, and an ugly color you're not allowed to paint over. Here are two different fabric-based coverups that help disguise a wall that needs it. Depending on the state of your walls, you may want to whip up extra-large versions of both.

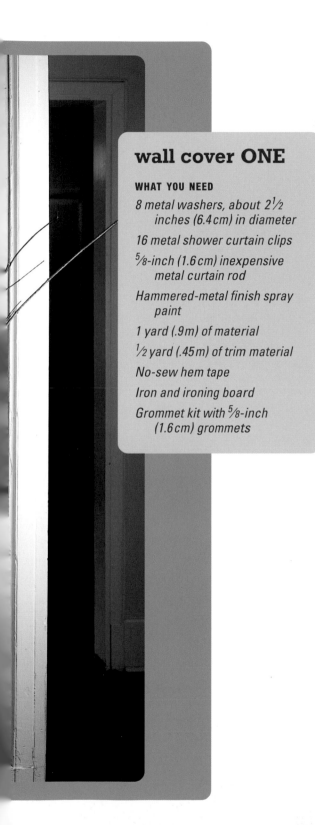

wall cover ONE

WHAT YOU NEED

8 metal washers, about 2½ inches (6.4 cm) in diameter

16 metal shower curtain clips

⅝-inch (1.6 cm) inexpensive metal curtain rod

Hammered-metal finish spray paint

1 yard (.9 m) of material

½ yard (.45 m) of trim material

No-sew hem tape

Iron and ironing board

Grommet kit with ⅝-inch (1.6 cm) grommets

WHAT YOU DO

1 Spray the washers, shower curtain clips, curtain rod and hardware, and grommets with the hammered-metal paint. Let the pieces dry.

2 Cut your larger piece of fabric to the length and width you want, keeping in mind that the finished piece will be approximately 8 inches (20.3 cm) longer with the trim and hanging hardware.

3 Following the directions on the packaging, use the hem tape to finish off the sides of the large piece.

4 Cut two 8-inch (20.3 cm) strips of the trim fabric, making the strips about 2 inches (5.1 cm) longer than the width of the main fabric panel. Fold over the short ends of both strips, and hem them with the hem tape. Make sure the finished length of the two strips matches exactly the width of the main fabric piece.

5 Fold the trim strips in half lengthwise, and press them. Fold the raw edges into the pressed crease, and press again.

6 Place the main fabric on the ironing board. Fit one trim strip over one end of the main fabric, making sure the ends line up, with no overhang, and that the fabric is straight. Attach the strip with hem tape. Attach the other strip to the other end of the main fabric, following the same process.

7 Use the grommet kit and the instructions that come with it to attach grommets to the top and bottom of the wall hanging. Make sure they're evenly spaced and all the same distance from the edge of the hanging.

8 Attach shower clips through the grommets. Thread the curtain rod through the clips at the top of the hanging. Attach the washers through the clips at the bottom.

9 Hang the piece with the curtain rod hardware.

wall cover TWO

You can, of course, simply hang purchased batik panels or tapestries inside old window frames. But if you want to make your own, scan the Batik Primer box below and follow the steps on page 71.

BATIK PRIMER

Batik is a way to resist-dye fabric, with wax serving as the resist. You pour or brush melted wax onto fabric. When it cools, it hardens in position and repels the dye. If you start with undyed fabric, the fabric's original color becomes part of your design. You can also wax areas that have been dyed already, and overdye them. Let's say you wax a circle on a white panel, then immerse the panel in yellow dye. Remove the wax, and you've now got a yellow panel with a white circle on it. Then, suppose you wax a triangle next to the circle and immerse the panel in blue dye. Remove this wax, and you now have a green panel with a white circle and a yellow triangle.

As you can see, this mixing of colors is the fun part, but it also takes some thinking ahead. Take a look at the color wheel on page 108 to figure out what color you get when you mix any other two together, then plot out your color sequence on a piece of paper before you start.

WHAT YOU NEED

Photocopies of images you want to transfer (optional)

Cold-water dyes in as many colors as your design calls for

Panels of 100-percent cotton fabric

Charcoal pen or chalk

Newspaper

Wax (Most craft stores sell batik wax. You need enough to create about 1 cup [240mL] of melted wax.)

Wax paper

Grocery bags

Mix of half water and half vinegar in a misting bottle (optional)

Salvaged frame (window frame, picture frame, etc.)

Hangers for frame

Pushpins

Wax melter (You need a way to heat the wax slowly without over-heating it. An electric skillet or small deep-fat fryer with a ther-mostatic heat control is ideal, but you'll need to use it for noth-ing other than wax melting. You can also use a double boiler.)

Several small paintbrushes or a tjanting tool (Tjantings, sold in art stores, have small metal reservoirs that hold the hot wax and heat-proof wooden handles. They create fine, precise lines of wax. They're not expensive, but they're also not essential.)

Iron

Hammer

Drill and drill bits (optional)

 If you use paintbrushes to apply your wax, they won't be usable for other purposes, so just let them cool off in the wax, then heat them up and reuse them for another batik project later.

Some of the wax you apply will crack, creating a spidery or cracked-glass effect where it does. This is part of the charm of batik, not a mistake. In fact, if you really like it, you can encourage cracking by wadding up your waxed fabric before you dye it.

WHAT YOU DO

1 Either sketch out the images you want to transfer to your fabric panels, or cut out the photocopied images you've chosen. Plan the color sequence you want to use when you dye.

2 With charcoal or chalk, transfer the images to the fabric.

3 Mix your dyes according to their package instructions.

4 Cover your work area with newspaper.

5 Melt the wax. It's ready when it flows like water. Test it on a scrap of fabric. If it looks transparent and it saturates the fabric thoroughly, it's ready. If it still looks milky on the fabric, it's not hot enough.

6 Put a piece of wax paper between the newspaper and your fabric, and apply your first layer of wax to certain elements of your design, using a paintbrush or a tjanting. Because wax dries quickly, you need to work quickly. Be sure it saturates the fabric.

7 Saturate the fabric in the first dye, then hang it to dry. Turn the heated wax off while the fabric is drying.

8 When you're ready for the next layer, reheat the wax, paint it over the next elements of your design, saturate the fabric in the second dye, and hang it to dry. Continue this process until you've completed the sequence you mapped out.

9 Once the final dye has dried, put the cloth between two pieces of brown grocery bags (printed side facing away from the wax), set your iron on high, and iron the cloth (with the bags providing protection) until all the wax is soaked up by the bags. If the bags become too saturated as you iron, replace them.

10 Once all the wax is completely removed from the fabric, you can further set your dyes by spritzing the fabric with the water-vinegar mixture and ironing it directly with your iron set on medium high.

11 Hang your frame, using either a hammer and picture-hanging nails or screws and a drill, depending on the size and weight of your frame.

12 Pin the fabric to the wall inside the frame.

floors

You come into immediate, physical contact with your floor every single day. If you hit the jackpot and you're traipsing around on pristine-condition hardwood, skip ahead. If not, here are ways to cover, color, accent, and modernize your area underfoot.

canvas floor cover

Why not pad around on your own little patch of personalized art? This one features a collage of fabric remnants, but you can also paint, sponge, stencil, or stamp on canvas to make lightweight, durable, one-of-a-kind floor covers.

WHAT YOU NEED

Prehemmed canvas (Art and craft stores carry them in a range of sizes.)

Liquid fabric dye in a color of your choice

Fabric remnants cut into rectangles measuring about 4½ x 5 inches (11.4 x 12.7 cm)

Fabric glue

Polyurethane sealer

Iron

Small sponge brush

Small scissors or nail clippers

Large nylon paintbrush

 Use warm soapy water and a sponge to spot clean your floor cover when it needs it.

WHAT YOU DO

1 Dye your canvas in a washing machine, following the directions on the dye packaging. Dry and iron the canvas.

2 Arrange the fabric remnants on the canvas. Eyeballing the arrangement rather than perfectly measuring the placement of each piece gives the floor cover a more casual feel.

3 With the sponge brush, spread an even layer of fabric glue on the back of each remnant, then flip each over and set it back in place on the canvas. Smooth the front sides of the remnants, adding more fabric glue to the tops of the pieces, if necessary.

4 Stand back and take a look. Rearrange any pieces that need it, then let the fabric glue dry.

5 Use the scissors or nail clippers to clip any frayed strings on the remnant edges.

6 Apply a thin coat of polyurethane to the surface of the floor cover with the large nylon paintbrush. Let it dry completely, then add a second coat.

mod floor modules

Seagrass squares come in sewn-together sets you can snip apart or stitch to others to create a floor covering that's the size and shape you need—that much the salespeople at the home decorating stores that carry them can tell you. What they may not know is that the muted, neutral colors those squares come in can be livened up in no time with paint and cardboard stencils.

WHAT YOU NEED

Seagrass squares (They're sold at home-decorating stores and through catalogs, typically in sets of six or so sewn together. Buy as many as you need to create a floor cover that's the size you want.)

Yellow acrylic latex, semigloss (About 1 quart [.95 L] should be enough.)

Red spray paint, semigloss or high gloss, 1 can

Black acrylic paint, 1 tube

2 cardboard squares (One should be the same size as your seagrass squares; the other can be slightly smaller.)

2 guides for drawing circles (glasses, bowls, etc.), one that will make a circle about 1½ inches (3.8 cm) larger in diameter than the other

Drop cloth

Small scissors (optional)

Needle and sturdy upholstery thread (optional)

2 paintbrushes, 1 large and 1 small

Craft knife

WHAT YOU DO

1 If necessary, snip the string holding your seagrass squares together or attach sets of squares to one another, using the needle and upholstery thread, to come up with a floor cover that's the size and shape you want.

2 Dilute the yellow paint, one-to-one, with water.

3 Using the large paintbrush, apply yellow paint to the front, back, and edges of the floor cover. Allow the paint to saturate the fibers, and then dry completely.

4 Use your smaller circle guide to mark a circle in the center of the larger cardboard square. Cut it out with the craft knife. The square with the cutout becomes your template for spraying red dots on each seagrass square.

5 Begin at the center of your floor cover and work outward. Place the cardboard template on a seagrass square, and spray red paint in the cutout circle area. Repeat until you've painted all the squares with red dots. Let the paint dry.

6 Create a second template from the smaller cardboard square. Mark a circle in the center using the larger circle guide, and cut it out.

7 To paint the black rings, go back to the center of your floor cover. Place the smaller cutout circle (from step 4) over the red dot to mask it, and center your new template around it. Press both cardboard pieces firmly in place, and paint the space in between with the black paint, using the small brush. Repeat until you've painted black rings around all the red dots. Let the paint dry.

Templates for painting the red dots and black rings

Buy a few extra seagrass squares, and paint place mats or trivets to match your floor cover.

rubber mat
kitchen floor

You spent all that time fantasizing about gathering with your friends in your snazzy new kitchen to sip, chat, and whip up fabulously cosmopolitan meals. Now, you're faced with the ugly reality—linoleum in rust or avocado green that looks as if people have been standing on it and throwing together tuna-noodle casseroles for years. Believe it or not, your vision can still be salvaged. Quite easily, as a matter of fact.

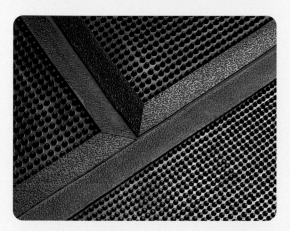

With their utilitarian appeal, rubber floor coverings can instantly modernize the most hopeless of surfaces. You'll find industrial-size rubber mats at restaurant supply outlets; they'll make your floor fit for the best of chefs, should you happen to know some. Or, you can simply use heavy-duty tape, as we did here, to connect the back side of several door mats, creating an urban-look floor cover that fits the size and shape of your space exactly.

first rites

Blessing a new dwelling is an ancient custom practiced the world over. Does it evict the negative energy of previous tenants or portend a comfortable future for you and yours? Maybe. But appropriately christening a new space definitely offers the psychological benefit of a fresh start. Here are some ideas to pick and choose from to create a ceremony that suits you.

CHARMS. Purify your home with natural items. Lay thorny branches near your doorstep, hang a sprig of seaweed in the kitchen, or place lilacs here and there. All are said to dispel evil spirits. A jar of alfalfa in a kitchen cupboard invites prosperous energy to the home. Fresh bamboo is thought to do the same. A sprinkle of sugar or salt (sprinkled, not spilled) is believed to cleanse a room of negative energies.

CLEANING. Unlike an aura, dirt is a residue everyone can see. Clean your new apartment thoroughly. Open all windows and doors, and let in lots of fresh air. Light scented candles and your favorite incense when you're finished, to infuse your new space with the aroma of spices and flowers of your choosing.

CUSTOMS. Many religions have house blessings. Native Americans of the Blackfoot tribe burn sage to purify and cleanse a space. An ancient Hebrew blessing instructs you to bring bread, water, salt, and a candle from your previous living space, make saltwater and sprinkle some on the bread, then light the candle. Improvise a verbal blessing, and take the candle to each window of the apartment. Let the candle shine out each window for a few seconds, then mark the windowsill with the saltwater. Mark all of the doorposts with the saltwater, too. Finally, eat the bread, and return to your old home before moving in.

HERBS. Use the fragrance of herbs to evoke specific moods. Hang a sprig of chamomile (a calming herb) to combat the chaos of unpacking. Let the invigorating scent of cedar bring you strength for all the activity. If you've taken the time to cast out bad spirits, set out eucalyptus oil or leaves to keep them (and, according to folklore, criminals) out. A pinch of thyme eaten before sleep is supposed to bring you good dreams. Why not try it for your first night in your new home?

checkerboard floor

If your landlord says it's okay to splash some paint on your apartment's wood floor (highly possible if it already features a paint job), you've got three choices. You can replicate exactly the bold, graphic pattern shown here. You can scale down this idea and create a painted-in-place checkerboard rug. Or, you can forget this design entirely, and simply use the techniques we describe to paint on a pattern you have in mind—or to roll on a solid color.

WHAT YOU NEED

Wood stripper and/or methylated spirit (optional)

Undercoat or primer

Paint (See page 25 for info on types.)

Roller and brushes

Varnish

Floor polisher (You can rent one at a grocery store. If you're painting only a small area, you can also polish by hand-sanding.)

Pencil

Tape measure and ruler

Chalk line (A handy, inexpensive tool that snaps straight lines. You can get one at a home improvement store. Step 4 tells you how to use it.)

Painter's tape (It's usually blue; you can buy it where you buy your paint.)

A friend who's willing to help (optional)

WHAT YOU DO

1 If the floor has already been painted and you're just painting over it, there's no need to strip the floor. If the floor has simply been varnished or polished, you need to strip the varnish or polish off with wood stripper or by scrubbing it with methylated spirit.

2 Sand the floor lightly just to smooth it; don't try to even out cracks or dents. Vacuum up the residue.

3 Roll on the undercoat, and let it dry.

4 Find the exact center of your floor, so you can mark out your diagonal checkerboard pattern from there. First, measure and lightly mark the center of each wall. Then, connect the marks on opposite walls by snapping a chalk line (see figure 1). To snap the lines, shake the reel, so the chalk inside distributes itself all over the string. Pull out the string and have a friend hold it close to the floor (but not touching) at one mark. (You can also attach the hook at the end of the string around a nail driven at the mark, if you're working alone.) Walk to the opposite mark, unreeling the string as you go. Pull the string taut, lower it to the floor, reach out a couple of feet, and give the string a snap. When it comes down, it'll leave a straight chalk line across the floor

5 From the center point, measure out an equal distance on each of the four lines, and mark those points. If you want to end up with 12-inch (30.5 cm) squares, for example, measure out 8½ inches (21.6 cm). Use the ruler and a light pencil line to connect the four points (see figure 2).

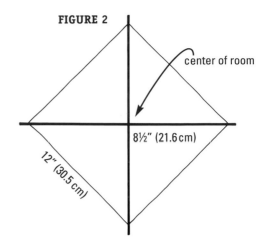

FIGURE 2

center of room

8½" (21.6 cm)

12" (30.5 cm)

6 The square you created in step 5 becomes your center "tile." Extend the lines of this tile out to the walls (again, snapping chalk lines is probably the easiest way), and finish marking off the rest of your squares.

7 Use painter's tape to tape off the inside lines of every other square (all the squares you want white, for example).

8 Paint all the black squares. The painter's tape will serve as an edge guard. Remove the tape, and let the paint dry.

9 Tape off the inside lines of all the black squares you just painted, and paint the white squares. Remove the tape, and let the white paint dry.

10 After the paint is completely dry, varnish the floor, following the varnish manufacturer's directions. You should probably apply several coats, depending on how much wear you expect the floor to take. Again, follow the manufacturer's directions on how long to wait between coats.

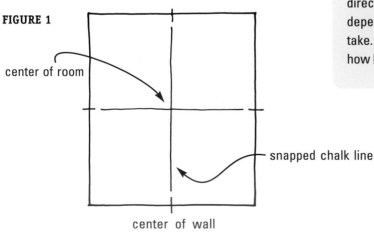

FIGURE 1

center of room

snapped chalk line

center of wall

getting to know your neighbors
(and why)

For people who don't actually live with you, your neighbors have enormous potential to affect whether your daily life is pleasant or not. That's why it's important to get a feel for your neighborhood—before you move in, if possible.

1 IMMEDIATE NEIGHBORS
Try to meet a few of your immediate neighbors (those in your hall and/or those living above or below you) face-to-face by knocking on their doors and introducing yourself. They'll be able to tell you from personal experience about the manager, the landlord, local amenities, other neighbors, and the general living situation in the building.

2 THE BUILDING
Walk around the inside and outside of the building. Is the cleanliness up to your standards? Do residents seem to turn common areas into extensions of their storage spaces (kayaks in the lobby, garbage bags in the hall)? Best to think about whether this bothers you now. Does it seem to be full of activity (maybe lots of small playing children or lots of grown-ups playing musical instruments) or relatively quiet? Consider which atmosphere suits your lifestyle.

3 THE NEIGHBORHOOD
Walk through the neighborhood around the apartment. Junk piles, graffiti, or folks loitering are generally deterrents for a prospective renter. Clean sidewalks, well-tended yards or storefronts, and neighbors conversing with one another suggest a sense of pride and security. If you'll be running or walking for exercise, taking a pet outdoors, or regularly coming home late at night, think about whether you'll feel comfortable carrying out those activities.

WHAT ABOUT YOU?
Evaluate your lifestyle. What kind of neighbor are you? Do you prefer living around families, college students, or young working professionals? Do you like to chat or prefer to mind your own business? If you're a night owl, don't live next door to children who spend the mornings playing outside your window. If you cherish your privacy, don't live in an apartment with a shared bath or shared kitchen privileges.

ONCE YOU'RE IN
As soon as potential neighbors become actual neighbors, it's in your best interest to start acting neighborly. Introduce yourself when you run into other renters at the mailboxes or in the parking lot. Sometimes apartment complexes host social gatherings for residents. Go, and get to know people. If you host your own apartment warming (see page 103), invite your immediate neighbors. These people can become pet sitters and plant waterers when you're away and sources of shared information about building maintenance or safety issues. They'll also likely become everything from business contacts to good friends.

Q U I C K F I X

problem

Water-warped wood or linoleum, grimy tile, or—heaven forbid—a carpet-covered bathroom floor.

quick fix

Head to a local garden center, and buy a few of the precast pavers made for laying out a garden path. Bring them back and scatter them strategically so they cover stains, add personality, or provide wet, just-washed feet with a clean place to step. You'll be able to find pavers in squares, circles, hexagons, and other standard shapes, and in a variety of colors and materials, from pressed aggregate (it looks like a bunch of little pebbles all bunched together) to simulated stone. One word of caution: when you place your pavers about, give some thought to whether bare toes might come up against them in the dark of night.

windows

Even if you lucked out and rented a room with an actual view, there are still going to be times you'll want to block it to shade the light or give yourself some privacy. Nice if you can do that in a way that adds to the indoor view, too.

word curtain

Your favorite word spelled out in five languages, the song lyrics that describe how you feel about life these days, or your funniest fortune-cookie predictions—you'll have no trouble finding the raw material for your own version of this printed-word window panel.

WHAT YOU NEED

Curtains
(You can use cotton muslin, if you're up to hemming the ends yourself, or plain, ready-made, rod-pocket curtain panels. Purchase fabric or panels that are somewhat longer and wider than the window you want to cover.)

Pencil and paper

Tacks or pushpins

MATERIALS FOR APPLYING LETTERING; OPTIONS INCLUDE:

Letter stencils, stencil brush, and acrylic paints (Block-letter stencils on manila paper are the easiest to use.)

Rubber stamps and ink pads

Fabric markers

Enlarged photocopies of words and a transfer medium (Check art and craft stores. You can buy bottles of medium that you apply with a brush and blender pens that allow you to transfer a photocopied image by burnishing it.)

WHAT YOU DO

1 On a piece of paper, sketch out the words and layout you have in mind. (Now would also be the time to check your spelling.)

2 Working on a hard, flat surface, lightly pencil guidelines onto the fabric, if you want them. If you'll be printing a poem on the fabric, for example, you might want the lines to be straight. If you're printing single words, on the other hand, maybe you'd rather they be more randomly placed (unless you're using the words *obsessive* or *compulsive*).

3 Print your words onto the fabric, using one of the following techniques.

- Tape letter stencils together to form your words, and stencil them onto the fabric, applying acrylic paint with a stencil brush. In addition to block-letter stencils, you can find letter stencils in cursive and other fancy forms. You can also trace the stencils with fabric markers if you don't want to stencil with a brush and paint.

- Stamp out your words using rubber-stamp alphabets and dye-based or craft inks. Avoid using pigment inks for this project.

- Use permanent fabric markers, and write on the fabric freehand—an especially good idea if you know calligraphy, have a distinctive handwriting style, or have a friend with exceptionally good penmanship who's willing to help. For large-scale, graphic lettering, you can also try writing on blank paper, enlarging the script on a photocopier, and tracing the result.

- Enlarge and make mirror-image copies of a printed page from a dictionary, a book of poetry, or anything else that strikes your fancy. Use a transfer medium to apply the image to the fabric, following the directions on the transfer medium's packaging.

4 Hang your printed panel on a curtain rod (if you used a curtain panel with a rod pocket), or use tacks or pushpins to attach it to the wall above your window.

emergency supply kit

Here are some essential items you might need when your karma runs out (or the power goes off, a snowstorm hits, or you find yourself in some other sort of bind). At the risk of sounding like your father: if you have it, you probably won't need it; if you don't, you'll wish you did. If you like to be super prepared, assemble an emergency kit. Otherwise, at least keep everything well stocked, close at hand, and in a location you can remember.

- Batteries
- Battery-powered clock or watch
- Battery-powered radio
- Candles
- Can opener
- Chocolate (hide it well)
- Duct tape
- Emergency money (for REAL emergencies, not a great poker hand!)
- Escape ladder* (if you live on the ground floor, you can skip this one)
- Extra prescription medication

- Flashlight (one that works)
- Fire extinguisher*
- First aid instruction book
- First aid kit (available premade at your local pharmacy)
- Instant cold pack
- Lighter
- Matches (in a waterproof container)
- Scissors
- Sharp knife
- Smoke detector* (DO NOT ever remove the batteries.)

- In-case-of-emergency phone list: nearest fire department, hospital, landlord, plumber, doctor, power company, phone com-pany, your family's phone number(s), roommate's family's number(s), your phone number and address (in case someone else has to make the call), vet (if your apartment includes residents with fur or feathers), favorite pizza place, your astrologer/psychic consultant

*These items should be provided by your landlord.

IF YOU LIVE IN A REGION WHERE THE TEMPERATURE DIPS BELOW FREEZING, BE SURE TO INCLUDE:

- Non-electric heater
- Extra blankets and wool socks
- High-protein emergency food
- Instant hot chocolate
- Snow shovel
- Rock salt or kitty litter (to make icy steps less dangerous)

IF YOU LIVE IN A REGION WHERE THE MERCURY OFTEN AIMS FOR THE TOP OF THE THERMOMETER, BE SURE TO INCLUDE:

- Handheld fan
- Box fan
- Instant lemonade
- Instant cold packs (enough to cover your entire body at once)
- Plane tickets to the frozen wastelands of the north

problem

Boxy windows, a boring view of the neighboring building, drab drapes you can't afford to replace, or a devastating combination of all three.

quick fix

Okay, so they're not going to transform your cube-shaped city windows into floor-to-ceiling sliding doors that offer an ocean view, but curtain rods with a bit of character can help perk up your outlook. They're also a lasting investment; when you move on, you take them with you. Home decorating shops and catalogs sell rods made of everything from brushed pewter to antique brass. They also carry finials (those ornamental stoppers on the ends) in all sorts of styles. For a more industrial look, here's an easy do-it-yourself option. Cut copper pipe to size with a hack saw, and hang it from I bolts or coat hooks (top). Or, connect the ends of the pipe to elbow-style plumbing fixtures you can screw into the wall on either side of the window (right and below).

standing sheers

There are lots of reasons—light, drama, distinctive style—that you might want gauzy veils covering your windows rather than big, old, heavy drapes. These fanciful standing panels can move from window to window or room to room, and you can find everything you need to make them at a home improvement store.

WHAT YOU NEED

Sheer panels (Buy them in stores that sell curtains.)

1¼-inch round wooden rods, 2 per panel (This is the most common-size wooden rod sold at home improvement stores. It's possible to find smaller-diameter rods if you want them, but it may take a few phone calls to locate them.)

2½-quart (2.4 L) metal paint pails, 2 per panel

Small bag of quick-setting concrete

Screw eyes, 2 per panel

2-inch (5.1 cm) loose-leaf book rings, 10 per panel

Measuring tape or ruler

Handsaw (optional)

Grommet kit with ½-inch (1.3 cm) grommets

Hammer

Nails

Plastic bucket for mixing concrete

Masking or duct tape

WHAT YOU DO

1 Measure the height and width of the space you want to cover with your panels, jot down the measurements, and take them with you to purchase what you'll need. You may have to buy more than one panel to cover the width of the space. If so, increase the numbers of your other supplies accordingly. Select wooden rods that are equal to or slightly taller than the height of your panels. You may have to cut them to height with a handsaw. Unless you're absolutely sure of your measurements, it's best to cut the rods at home rather than having them cut at the store.

2 Set a grommet in both upper corners of each panel, following the instructions that come with the grommet kit. Then, lay one panel on a flat surface. Mark the positions for four equally spaced grommets down one long side, and set the grommets. Repeat on the other side.

3 Lay a second panel, if you're creating more than one, alongside the first. Mark identical grommet positions down each side of the second panel, and set them as you did on the first panel. Align the panels to be certain that the grommets line up as closely as possible. Continue with as many panels as you have.

4 Use a hammer and nail to punch a small hole in the center of one of the paint pail bottoms. Stand a rod in the pail, and nail it in place. Nail rods in all the other pails, using the same process. Don't worry if the rods wiggle a bit. The nails are simply to help steady them as you pour in the concrete mix.

5 Take the rods and pails outdoors. (Don't attempt to mix concrete on carpet or hardwood floors; you'll regret it.) Follow the manufacturer's instructions for mixing the concrete in the plastic bucket. Pour the mix into each pail almost but not quite up to the rim. If necessary, you can steady the rod with tape to keep it standing straight until the concrete mix sets. Allow the concrete to harden.

6 Place a screw eye at the top of each rod (see the photo below).

7 Open a loose-leaf ring, and thread it through the top grommets of two panels. Bring each end of the ring through the screw eye, and snap them together.

8 Anchor the sides of the panels by connecting the grommet holes with the rings.

9 Connect all your panels, following this same process.

picture window

Transform the overflow from someone's camera-happy vacation into a window treatment that both flutters and casts color. Look for boxes of transparent slides selling for next to nothing at yard sales, or ask for the contents of the reject bin at your local photo finishing place.

WHAT YOU NEED

Transparent slides

Small S hooks

Decorative curtain rod with ends in a size that fits your window

O rings with clips (Look for them with curtain rods and ends.)

Tape measure

Hack saw (optional; only if you need to cut your curtain rod to size)

Leather punch

Needle-nose pliers

WHAT YOU DO

1 If necessary, cut your curtain rod to fit the width of your window.

2 Measure the window's length, and lay out slides to figure a rough estimate for the number you'll need for each "strand." (Once you make your first strand, you'll know exactly how many slides and S hooks you'll need for each.)

3 Start punching holes in the slides to create as many strands as you need. First, orient each slide image so it's upright, then center the holes in the top and bottom edges of the slide casing. Work gently and slowly as you punch, or you'll split and crack the slide casings.

4 Use the S hooks to connect the slides into vertical strands, squeezing the curved ends of each hook together with the needle-nose pliers. Don't worry about completely closing the hooks, just squeeze them enough that they won't come loose from the slides.

5 Slip the O rings on the curtain rod, and use their clips to hold the top slide in each strand.

 On the top slide in each strand, punch only the bottom hole. On the bottom slide, punch only the top hole.

no-sew exotica curtain

Why in the world would you hang a boring, pre-fab curtain over the focal-point window in your living room (or even over the nearly hidden window in your bathroom), when draping it in silk and beads is such a snap?

WHAT YOU NEED

Piece of fabric to fit your window (See page 28 to measure for curtain size. The key to keeping this easy is to work with the fabric's existing width—typically 45 inches [114.3cm]—and have it cut about 1½ inches [3.8cm] longer than you need, so you can hem the ends. If your window is wider than the fabric, use supple fabric that can be bunched together, and make more than one curtain.)

Fusible web

Length of ⅞-inch (2.2 cm) grosgrain ribbon, slightly longer than your curtain is wide

Supply of straight pins

#8 silk beading cord (comes with a wire "needle" attached to it)

1 large bead and 1 seed bead per dangle on the curtain's bottom edge

Tapestry needle

Curtain clips

Curtain rod and hanging hardware

Iron and ironing board

Scissors

Ruler or tape measure

WHAT YOU DO

1 Your piece of fabric will have two finished edges (known as selvege edges in the sewing world) and two unfinished or raw edges. The finished edges are your curtain's sides. The unfinished edges, which you'll hem with fusible web, are the top and bottom. With the fabric right side up, fold either the top or bottom edge over ¾-inch (1.9cm), so the right sides of fabric are together, and press the fold. Open the fold, and place a strip of fusible web as long as your curtain is wide above the fold line. Fold the fabric back over onto the fusible web, and iron it down, following the fusible web manufacturer's instructions.

2 Cut the grosgrain ribbon in two equal lengths, each a couple of inches (5.1cm) longer than the width of your curtain.

3 Cut another strip of fusible web as long as your curtain is wide. Line up one edge with the edge of the hem you created in step 1. Place the ribbon over the fusible web, leaving equal amounts of extra ribbon on either side. Iron the ribbon down, following manufacturer's instructions. Flip the fabric over, and use short lengths of fusible web to attach the extra allowance of ribbon onto the back of the curtain.

4 Repeat steps 1 through 3 to hem the other end of the curtain.

5 You'll bead one of the hems to make it the curtain's bottom. Mark 2½-inch (6.4 cm) intervals from one side to the other with pins.

6 Unwind all the silk cord from its spool, and tie a knot in the end that doesn't have the wire attached to it. Using the wire, thread the silk through the tapestry needle. Push the needle through the fabric from the back to the front at one of the pins, about ¼ inch (6mm) up from the hem edge. Pull all the thread through, and remove the needle. Using the wire, thread a big bead, then a seed bead. Go back up through the bottom of the big bead and pull the thread through, adjusting it so the beads hang ¼ inch (6mm) below the hem. Thread the silk onto the upholstery needle again, pull the needle and thread through the ribbon hem, from the front to the back, and tie off, being careful not to pull so tightly that the beads no longer dangle below the edge of the hem.

7 Repeat step 6 to attach all your other dangles. Two of them should be on the very edges of the curtain.

8 Attach the curtain clips evenly along the top hem of the curtain, install the rod, and hang it.

problem

You've got a window in dire need of some dressing up, but it's also one of your dark apartment's few sources of natural light, so there's no way you're going to cover it with curtains.

quick fix

Transform your window's panels into faux stained glass. All you need are sheets of colored tissue paper or cellophane, some scissors to cut them to size, and spray adhesive to hold the cut shapes in position on the window's glass. If you've got a multipaned window, fill each section with a different color—maybe alternating mauve and blue, a gradation of green, or a random collage of colors, some layered on top of each other. If your window features one big pane of glass, instead, fill the center with your own design of colored geometric shapes. Nail polish remover will take off any spray adhesive residue left behind when you decide to peel off the colored sheets.

decorative pull

You can live with the simple shades or blinds that were already covering your apartment's windows when you moved in, but your tolerance for minimalism goes only so far. Those plain hanging cords that control them cry out for something more substantial to feel for in the dark (or something more interesting for the cat to bat about while you're at work). Here's an easy reminder that it's the little things that make a home your own.

WHAT YOU NEED

Large, unpainted wooden beads (Look in craft stores.)

Acrylic paints

Acrylic varnish (spray or liquid)

Small brushes

Fine sandpaper

WHAT YOU DO

1 Thin the acrylic paint with water. Apply the thinned paint to the beads with a brush. Let the beads dry.

2 Sand the beads with fine sandpaper, then recoat them with more paint if they look like they need it. Feel free to add dots, swirls, squiggles, or stripes to your beads. Let them dry.

3 Coat the beads with acrylic varnish to protect them from wear.

4 Remove the plastic end from your cord pull by untying the knot that holds it on. Slip the beads onto the cord in its place, and tie off the end of the cord with a simple overhand knot.

If you are, by nature, more of a browser than a crafter, forget the wooden beads and paint. Instead, head straight to a bead store, where you can find pieces made of everything from carved bone to Austrian crystal to thread onto your personal pull.

lighting

Despite the fact that there are expansive stores and hefty catalogs devoted solely to the subject of lighting, it's no more complicated than this: you need it either to see what you're doing or to set a mood. Here are some options for shedding both types of light.

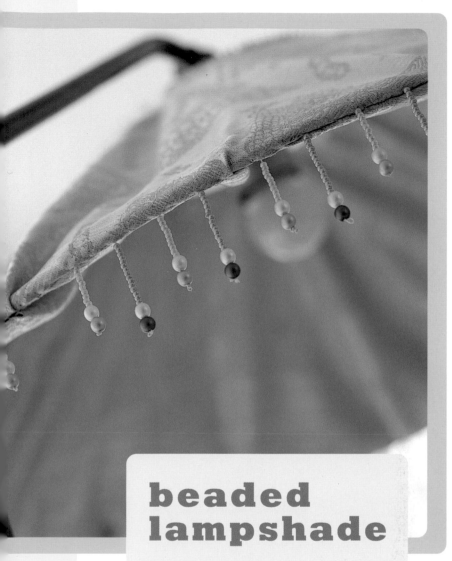

beaded lampshade

Now that most craft and fabric stores sell prebeaded and other types of decorative fringe, you can give any old lamp a touch of flapper-era shimmer, movie-star glamour, or Far Eastern mystery. All you'll need is glue or, if you're really feeling ambitious, a needle and thread and the simplest of sewing skills.

WHAT YOU NEED

Prebeaded fringe

Glue (options include a glue gun or white craft glue) or a needle and thread (Your choice of fastener depends on your shade; see step 2.)

Cloth tape measure or a length of string and a ruler

Scissors

WHAT YOU DO

1 To figure how much fringe to purchase, measure the circumference of the bottom of your shade. Either use a cloth tape measure, or wrap a length of string around the bottom of the shade, mark the string, then measure it with a ruler. The prebeaded fringe comes sewn onto a thin strip of fabric or ribbon. Buy a strip slightly longer than what you need.

2 Decide how you'll attach your fringe. You can glue fringe directly to the inner or outer edge of a paper or plastic shade with white glue or hot glue from a glue gun; hot glue is the easiest method. If you have a cloth-covered shade, you can glue the fringe or, if you're so inclined, stitch it to the shade with needle and thread.

3 Place the shade upside down on a flat work surface. Glue or stitch the fringe in small increments to either the inner or outer bottom edge of the shade. You'll have to hang the beads over the edge of the shade as you work. Keep the bottom edge of the fringe's fabric or ribbon strip parallel to the bottom edge of the shade.

4 Trim the end of the fringe strip so it butts up against the starting point. Turn the shade right side up, and check to make sure your fringe hangs evenly.

wastebasket glow lamps

Sources of direct, utilitarian lighting they're not. But if your goal is to set a mood or soften the harsh reality of unvacuumed carpet or undusted furniture, these radiating wastebaskets are just the thing.

The "O" decorating the wall just above the glow lamps is an old zinc letter that once helped spell out a company name on a building facade. If your local scrap yard is fresh out of the letters of the alphabet you need, home decorating catalogs now sell them brand new.

WHAT YOU NEED

Clear plastic wastebasket with a frosted finish, 1 per lamp

White craft glue

3 or 4 sheets of colored tissue paper per lamp

Small lamp (You need just the lamp apparatus, no shade. Thrift stores are a good place to find inexpensive lamps.)

Self-piercing plug to fit on the end of an electrical cord

Drill with ⅛-inch (3mm), ⅜-inch (9.5mm), and ¼-inch (6mm) drill bits

Small plastic container with lid

Paintbrush

Heavy-duty scissors

Screwdriver

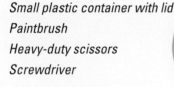

WHAT YOU DO

1 Drill a hole on one side of the wastebasket, near the bottom; start with a ⅛-inch (3mm) pilot hole, then drill that same hole with a ⅜-inch (9.5mm) bit , and finally drill it with a ¼-inch (6mm) bit.

2 Pour a solution of three parts glue to one part water into the plastic container. Mix it well with the paintbrush.

3 Cut the tissue paper into manageable sections slightly longer than the height of the wastebasket and about 6 inches (15.2cm) wide.

4 Brush glue onto a section of the interior of the waste-basket, and apply a strip of tissue paper. Use the brush to gently flatten the tissue paper and smooth out any air pockets. Keep applying the tissue paper in sections until the entire wastebasket is covered, again using the brush to push overlapping pieces into place. (Don't worry about tears in the paper; subsequent layers will hide them.) Let the glued paper dry overnight.

5 Trim off the top edges of the tissue paper, and use your finger and then glue to smooth any rough areas on the tissue paper. Repeat the process of applying glue and tissue paper, then allow it all to dry again.

6 Apply about three or more layers of tissue to the inside of the wastebasket, then add an extra coating of glue after the final layer of paper. Let everything dry once more.

7 Pierce through the hole in the wastebasket with the screwdriver, working from the outside of the basket in. Using heavy-duty scissors, cut the plug off the lamp cord, thread the cord through the hole, and attach a new plug, following the instructions on the plug's packaging. Place the lamp in the center of the wastebasket, and equip it with a low-wattage bulb.

problem

Stark, overhead ceiling lights that bathe your apartment in an unattractive, interrogation-like glare.

quick fix

Called *uplighters* in interior decorating-ese, freestanding lamps that sit low on the floor and cast light up are one of the quickest ways to give a bland room character. Position them behind plants, under tables or benches that hug a wall, or in corners, and they can create interesting shadows and reflections, light up entire walls to give the illusion of more space, highlight architectural angles or recesses, and even spotlight whatever is hanging above them.

plumbing parts candlesticks

Candlelight is something you're going to want to toss into your lighting mix every now and then, and how you hold the candles in place is a big part of the look you create. These candlesticks made from off-the-shelf plumbing parts will be right at home, whether you live in a converted-factory loft or simply like to pretend you do.

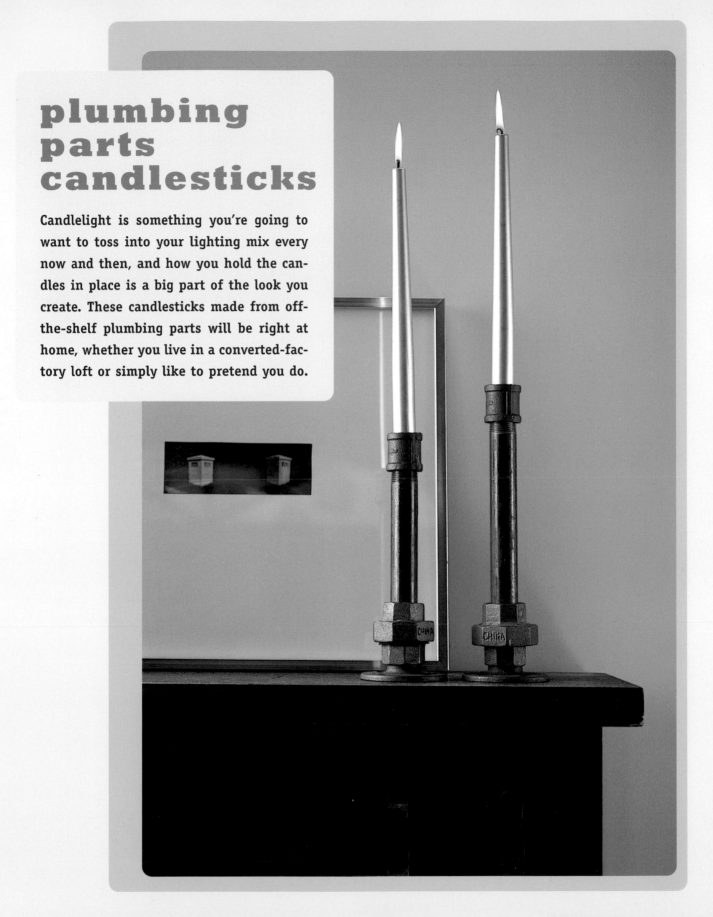

WHAT YOU DO

1 Screw one pipe into one flange to create the base of each candlestick.

2 Slide the couplings onto the pipes so they rest on the bases.

3 Screw the fittings to the top of each piece to add definition.

even easier...

We have no idea exactly what these super-cheap parts were manufactured to do, but we think they make terrific candlesticks. (The friendly fellow who helps customers maneuver their way through the plumbing aisle liked the idea, too.) The only assembly required: the addition of a taper candle.

candles by style

TRADITIONAL: Buy a wide wooden baluster at a furniture salvage store (these are the wooden support posts from old handrails). Spray paint it metallic gold or silver. Top it with a thick, chunky square or round candle. If you don't happen to have a baby grand piano, use this as an imposing centerpiece for your table.

ETHNIC: Wrap tall pillar candles halfway up with Oriental rice paper, African mud cloth, or remnant scraps of velvet or raw silk. Tie the wraps with raffia, tassels, or rope, and decorate the ties with beads, coins, or tokens. Roll the wraps down as the candles burn.

ECLECTIC: Group a bunch of mismatched candleholders you picked up in a thrift shop (colored glass, brass, painted wood, etc.), and fill them with candles in different sizes, shapes, and colors.

MINIMALIST: Settle white votive candles into shallow clear bowls filled with pebbles or sand, or use large, flat river rocks as candleholders.

KITSCH: Time to transform your Polynesian-mask cocktail mugs into candleholders, use an old surfboard as an oversized candle platter, or pose Barbie and Skipper so their arms appear to be holding your taper candles upright.

apartment-warming parties

SIX WAYS TO GIVE YOUR NEW HOME THE TOASTY GLOW
GOOD FRIENDS AND THEIR VIBES PROVIDE...

OPEN HOUSE. An especially good plan when you have more friends than chairs. Choose a Saturday or Sunday afternoon, and let guests know they're welcome to come and go anytime within a several-hour window. Set out a simple spread of finger foods and drinks—and make sure you have enough refills on hand to keep the refreshments looking fresh throughout your open-house hours.

POTLUCK. Nothing cozies up a new place like a big, home-cooked meal, especially when everyone who's coming contributes to the cooking. If your new kitchen is not yet overflowing with lots of extra dishes and flatware, make the place settings potluck, too. Invite everyone to bring one, then mix and match all the plates and utensils.

DINNER PARTY. This step up from a potluck is for those landmark times when you have not only a new apartment but also grown-up extras, such as cloth napkins and a set of wine glasses that you're eager to show off. Don't feel you have to go overboard; plan and budget for an appetizer, entree, salad, and a dessert, and you've got a multicourse evening. Though the idea is that you're providing the bulk of the food, it's fine to have guests fill in some gaps (bottle of wine, loaf of bread, etc.). Light some candles, splurge on a bouquet of fresh flowers, turn on some background music, and tell everyone to dress up.

COSTUME OR THEME PARTY. Perfect for establishing your apartment as the party place, one where guests can expect decorations and props, if not games, activities, food, and music to match the mood. If it's a costume party, have plain masks and decorating materials at the door for anyone who arrives in street clothes. Looking for an easy theme? Re-create a kid-style birthday party for a friend who's hitting a 20-something milestone (cupcake decorating contest, musical chairs with gag prizes, hats and horns). Feeling especially ambitious? Send out written theme invitations in advance.

DANCE PARTY. If you don't have lots of furniture to fill your floors, you might as well dance. Base your party on a memorable decade or fad (1950s, disco) or on a celebratory holiday such as Mardi Gras, costumes and all.

FOOD-THEME PARTY. Add focus and embellishment to any potluck or dinner party by setting up a theme buffet. Try make-your-own tacos, and you can also string a piñata, offer Mexican-hat-dance lessons, and have some sombreros handy for your more extroverted guests. Or, put out pita-bread pockets guests can fill with Greek salad as they mingle around in togas.

mini-lights

There are people in the world who believe that little tiny lights should be used only for wrapping around evergreen trees and plastic rein-deer—and only once a year. You should feel pity for them. Somehow, they've missed the news that these twinkling, blinking, inexpensive strings can be wound among the leaves of house plants, draped behind sheer curtains, mounded in clear glass containers, and used in countless other ways to provide year-round light and good cheer.

MINI-LIGHTS know exactly how to behave when they're strung among the leaves of something green. Group several small plants in front of an out-let, and use a short string of lights to make them sparkle. Or, turn a tall tree or plant into a living floor lamp. Weave the lights through the leaves and branches, then attach them to an exten-sion cord you can wind around the trunk and off to the outlet.

CREATE a quick table lamp by filling a big glass bowl, platter, pitcher, or urn with a strand of lights and nearly anything else: corks, glass marbles, seedpods, candy with bright-colored cellophane wrappers, or your collection of plastic Barbie doll shoes.

BACK in the aisles you perhaps never visit, home improvement stores sell these minimalist-look steel concrete reinforcement grids. Toss (okay, carefully lift) a couple into your back seat, take them home, and use them as free-standing frames for stringing lights. To make your display even more distinctive, shop thrift stores and antique shops for vintage bulbs like these.

problem

Though you may not have known it had an actual name (it does: task lighting), you do know you need more of it—a directed stream that highlights details when you're reading a book, choosing a CD, or writing in your journal.

quick fix

Clip-on lights will grip the edges of tables and counters, the top of a headboard, the side of a shelf, even the rim of a windowsill. Then, you can swivel them and train them on whatever it is you want to see— or on some decorative item you want to spotlight. Places that sell lighting fixtures carry all sorts of styles, but for good old-fashioned (not to mention inexpensive) metal clip-ons with a no-nonsense industrial edge, you can't beat your local hardware store.

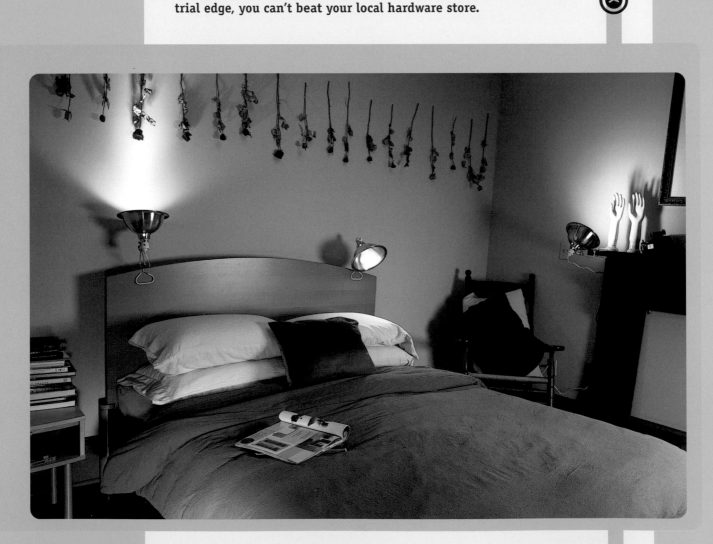

free-form mesh light fixtures

The standard-issue light fixtures in apartments are seldom unbearably bad. They're just boring. Fortunately, most of them can be removed with the simple twist of a few screws. Pack them away carefully, so you can reinstall them when it's time to collect your security deposit and move out. Meantime, here's a two-step plan for putting some pizzazz in their place.

1 Experiment with different bulbs, from round globes to bulbs with frosted and colored finishes. On this bathroom fixture, we replaced the regular bulbs with long, low-watt tubes.

2 Cover the bulbs with contour mesh. This malleable aluminum comes in various colors and finishes. It's sold by the roll at craft stores. Put on a pair of work gloves (the edges can be sharp), and twist, gather, sculpt, and shape it until you've fashioned a shade you like.

color your world

COLOR is one of your most effective and least expensive decorating tools. A coat of paint or a vibrant bouquet of flowers here, a few colored light bulbs there, and you can completely change the feel of a room. Here are the basics you need to splash color around with confidence.

A SPIN ON THE COLOR WHEEL
...or, what you forgot to remember from art class

PRIMARY COLORS

Red, blue, and yellow; pure colors that can't be mixed from others.

SECONDARY COLORS

Result of mixing two primary colors; you get violet, orange, or green.

HARMONIOUS COLORS

Colors adjacent to each other on the color wheel, such as red, red-orange, and orange.

COMPLEMENTARY COLORS

Colors opposite each other on the color wheel, such as red and green, orange and blue, and yellow and violet. When placed beside each other, they seem to vibrate. Also known as contrast colors, they are often used as accents in a color scheme.

COOL COLORS

Those that are more blue than red; they appear to advance.

WARM COLORS

Those that are more red than blue; they appear to recede.

NEUTRAL COLORS

Whites, blacks, grays, and browns. They're considered both "safe" and restful. They can vary considerably in warmth or coolness. At their purest, white is cool and black is warm.

COLOR IN THEORY

If you remember mood rings, you know that each color symbolizes something different. (This is not only according to the manufacturers of mood rings. People who actually study such stuff—known as color theorists—say so, too.) Here's a quick breakdown of the effects generally associated with various colors. Toss this info into the mix when you're picking out paints or rugs, but don't worry too much about rules. Better to imagine colors as having personalities, and choose those you connect with.

NEUTRALS

Imply good taste and elegance. Although they might seem understated, don't think of neutrals as bland. White is crisp, refined, clean. Black can represent dignity, serenity, and formality.

REDS

Warm and vibrant, red adds drama and cheer. If you're using lots of it, combine it with accents of white or cream to keep it crisp, or with black for a hint of Asian aesthetic. For an opulent room that's not for the faint-hearted, use only shades of red and deep golds. Mixed as an accent with other colors, red has a playful feel.

PINKS

Fresh and charming. Pastel pinks work well with other soft shades and sometimes feel nostalgic; mix hot pinks with amber, yellow, and coral shades for a taste of the tropics.

ORANGE

Said to stimulate the appetite, orange sometimes gets a bad rap as a faddish color that's hard to combine with others. In the right proportion, however, it can work well with its complements and with neutrals. It's dominant, lively, and fun, especially for bathrooms and work areas.

YELLOW

Bright and cheery, yellow is associated with intellect, power, and creative energy. Lighter, less-radiant shades of yellow are easiest to work with. Most people prefer yellow, like orange, as an accent only.

GREENS

Considered fresh and delicate, greens help reduce nervousness and tension. Dark greens work well in distinguished settings, while soft greens have the most soothing effect. If it were a person, green would be a valued guest at cocktail parties because it mixes so well with others!

BLUES

Evoking images of water, the sky, and nautical themes, blues are used to create harmonious, serene settings. Blues combine well with each other and can soften overly bright rooms. Also, cool blues and white are considered an especially refreshing pair.

VIOLETS

With their strong, majestic tones, violets are powerful accent colors. They also have multiple personalities; the look depends on what you mix them with.

COLOR SCHEMES

● To make a ceiling seem higher, paint your walls in vertical stripes, or, if you have a chair railing, paint the area below it darker than the area above.

● Rooms decorated in dark colors appear smaller than those furnished in light colors.

● To hide architectural flaws, paint a room in a single, distinctive color, which causes the eye to move around the room and not rest on any details.

● If you choose to paint rooms in different colors, use the same color trim to visually connect them all.

● Bear in mind that color is never static. Not only does a color change according to the quality of sunlight bathing it, but it looks different depending on the colors beside it.

furniture & accessories

You need something to sleep on, something to sit on, some surfaces on which to stack belongings, and a few items to serve as accents. Just because you're meeting all of these needs with a combination of hand-me-down pieces and bargain buys, there's no reason they can't look good.

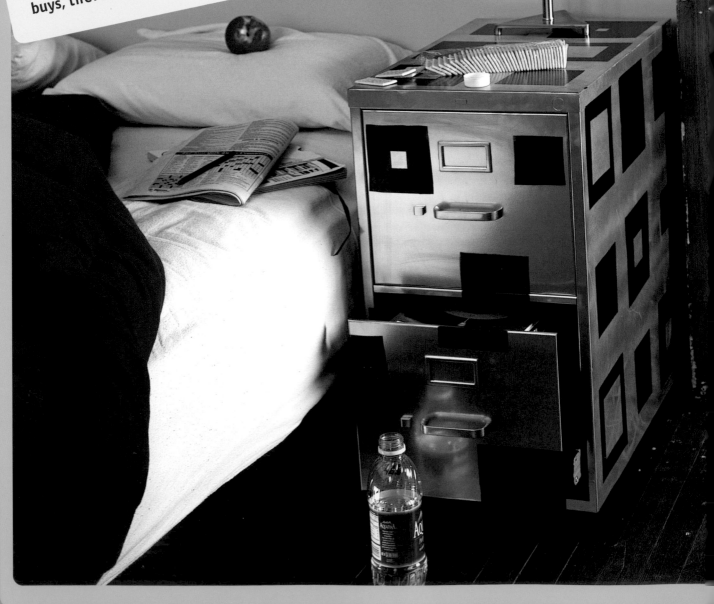

painted file cabinet

Some people use them to hold actual files (gotta put those college loan records and cat adoption papers somewhere). Others turn them into unconventional dresser drawers (complete with built-in slots for labeling each) or extra kitchen storage containers. But just because file cabinets are so versatile and easy to come by is no reason for yours to look ordinary.

WHAT YOU NEED

Painted File Cabinet Masking Patterns, page 156

File cabinet

1 can of spray paint (We used chrome on a black file cabinet.)

Acrylic paint that matches the color of your cabinet

Newspaper

Scissors

Masking tape

WHAT YOU DO

1 On a photocopier, enlarge the masking patterns to the size you want, and make 12 copies of each. Cut them out with scissors.

2 Attach the patterns in a random fashion to the cabinet, and spread them out evenly, making sure that the same patterns aren't right beside each other. Affix them with masking tape along the edges, making it as straight as possible, but don't worry if it's not perfect. This design is not about precision. Use your fingernail to press down the edges of the masking tape, so the paint won't spray under its edge.

3 Working outside if at all possible, set the cabinet on a protective layer of newspaper, and tape doubled layers of newspaper to all but one side of the filing cabinet.

4 Spray the uncovered side of the cabinet, following the manufacturer's instructions on the spray can. Let the paint dry completely, then spray a second coat.

5 Once the second coat is dry, cover the painted area with a doubled layer of newspaper, uncover a new side, and repeat step 4. Repeat this process until you've painted all four sides.

6 If necessary, use the acrylic paint to touch up any imperfections.

other ideas to file away

PAINT IT	USE IT FOR
Fire-engine red	CD collection
With over-sized daisies	Towels & toilet paper in the bathroom
Using fern leaves as stencils	Shoes, scarves, umbrellas & hats by the front door
Sheep	Nightstand; store books in the drawers
Random numbers	Phone table

Look Good, Feel Good:
FENG SHUI DECORATING

According to the ancient Chinese practice of feng shui, a misplaced bed can make you tired, clutter can cloud your thinking, and a backed-up sink can cause your career to stagnate, just like the water in the basin. On the other hand, if you apply a few basic principles for furniture arranging and decorating, they can help alleviate everything from stress and anger to blocked creativity and blood pressure problems.

The words feng shui, pronounced "feng shwa," "fung shui," or "fung shwa," depending on whether you're Mandarin, Cantonese, or English speaking, mean wind and water. They describe the practice of positioning objects so they take advantage of—and don't block—the chi or energy flowing through the environment. If you've visited a bookstore in the last decade or so, you know that the detailed principles and techniques of feng shui are hardly being hidden away as ancient secrets. Before you buy your own full-blown guide, here's an overview of what it's all about.

BASICS

● Any apartment or house has negative space. You counteract it by stimulating chi.

● Balancing of the five elements of wood, earth, water, fire, and metal can help bring balance to your living space and your mental and physical life.

● Each element relates to one or more directions in the home (north, south, east, or west). Certain colors, objects, shapes, and ideas exemplify the elements and are used to decorate the corresponding parts of the home. For example, water rules the northern part of the home. Activate that area's chi by using blue tones to decorate. You might also consider furnishing the area with a small table fountain or an aquarium. Detailed feng shui guides will spell all this out for you in charts.

DOS & DON'TS
Do:

● Decorate with art. It can be a potent souce of inspiration and can act as a catalyst for achieving goals.

● Organize and fix up. Physical clutter mirrors chaotic thinking, and lots of unfinished repair work (leaky faucets, wobbly table legs, etc.) can challenge wealth and happiness.

● Tackle work projects in bright, open spaces; they're more energetic.

● Move to more softly lit places when you need to relax or calm down.

● Use bright objects to enhance the energy level in dark corners and nooks.

● Arrange your bedroom symmetrically. Position the bed so it has a clear view of the door but isn't in line with it.

● Consider the energy of shapes. Curves, circles, and ovals are linked with creativity. Squares and rectangles represent organization and rational thinking and stimulate decision making.

● Decorate with tall, upright plants. They have strong, upward energy that counteracts draining energy.

● Place plants next to electrical units to counteract electromagnetic discharges.

● Create a physical barrier between work and home if you work out of your apartment. If you can't shut the work off in a separate room, use a screen or plants to separate it.

Don't:

● Create sharp edges and corners with your furniture placement; they cut off energy. Round out architectural edges with plants or fabrics.

● Place chairs or any seating with their backs to a door.

● Use loud colors or modern prints in the bedroom; they're not restful. You should also avoid lots of vivid color and stimulating decor where you eat, to ease digestion.

● Put up with dead plants or peeling paint near your front door. Keep your entranceway clean and orderly—it's the gateway to your private life. (A Western approach calls for the use of wind chimes near an exterior door, to create positive sounds.)

● Decorate with too much white or black. Use colorful throw rugs, plants, and recent photos to brighten the atmosphere. Avoid blank walls.

● Rely too much on artificial light. Also, consider buying full-spectrum light bulbs; they're the most similar to natural light. They do, however, cost three to five times what a standard bulb does.

nathalie's chair

Nathalie found this chair at a bargain price at a thrift store and had to have it. She fell in love with its excellent bones, but didn't want to live five minutes with its fabric. Though she'd never reupholstered anything before, she figured all she really needed to transform her prize find into the chair of her dreams was some great new fabric and a little common sense. Turned out, she was right. Here's her step-by-step report of how she did it.

WHAT YOU NEED

*Chair or other piece of furniture
    you want to recover (See step 1.)*

Upholstery fabric (See step 2.)

*Batting (optional) (The piece's existing batting—the
    stuffing underneath the fabric—may be in good
    enough shape to reuse; see step 3.)*

Straight pins or fabric chalk

*Steel upholstery tacks (Reusing the tacks you pulled off
    the furniture might seem thrifty, but they don' t go in
    straight if they' ve been bent during the removal
    process.)*

Cardboard or metal tack strips (optional)

*Tack puller (This handy gadget easily slips under uphol-
    stery tacks, so you can remove them with little effort.)*

*Lightweight upholstery hammer or regular hammer
    (Though a standard hammer will work, upholstery
    hammers have a magnetic tip that holds tacks on
    the end, so you won't smash your fingers trying to
    hold them in place while you hit them.)*

Scissors

WHAT YOU DO

1 If this is your first upholstering job, too, select simple-lined furniture. This 1950s-era chair has spare but elegant lines that allow the new fabric to take the spotlight. Before buying furniture you plan to reupholster, check to make sure the existing fabric is not sewn on but rather folds into place over the stuffing. Also, make sure the furniture is structurally sound—you don't want to invest all kinds of time in a piece that will quickly fall apart.

2 Choose your fabric carefully. It should be robust enough to withstand daily use, without being so heavy that you can't drape it easily around the furniture's frame. Make sure the fabric is wide enough to fit completely over the elements you're covering. And unless you want to put a lot of effort into matching them, avoid stripes and plaids in fabric patterns. You'll determine exactly how much fabric you need once you've removed the old fabric from the furniture and lined all the pieces in a row (see step 5).

3 Remove your furniture piece's legs, if possible, and begin removing the existing upholstery. The process is much like peeling an onion layer by layer. At each step, carefully examine the furniture to make sure which element is outermost, then remove it. A few suggestions:

- Keep notes as you go on the order of what you remove; you'll reverse it when you attach your new fabric.

- As you remove elements, whether legs, fabric, or batting, label them for reference, pinning a piece of paper with the name—*seat* or *front of backrest*, for example—and indicate the front or top of each. In the case of legs, label them and the body of the furniture lightly in pencil where it won't show, so you'll know which slot they screw back into when you' re ready to put them back on.

- Write down measurements related to the placement of decorative elements, such as buttons, so you can put them back where they belong.

- If there's a particularly tricky way in which something is attached, jot down that information, as well as explanations of where tacks should go. Make marks directly on the frame of the furniture if something has to be attached in a specific spot.

- If you remove any wooden elements, clean them when they're off the piece, to give them back their luster—and so you won't muck up your spiffy new fabric cleaning them later.

4 Once you've removed all the fabric, assess the condition of the batting. You may have to replace it. If so, use the same quality batting or better. If you're unsure about this, ask for advice at the upholstery section of a fabric store or at an upholstery supply shop.

5 Working in a well-lit area on a smooth, clean surface, lay the fabric pieces you've removed in a row, and press them flat with your fingers. (Don't iron the old fabric; you'll remove folds and creases you might find helpful in determining how to fold your new fabric to shape it correctly around the furniture frame.) Use the pieces as a guide for how much new fabric you need.

6 Lay out your new fabric on the same smooth, clean surface, and use the old fabric pieces as patterns for cutting. You can either pin them to the new fabric or trace them with fabric chalk. As you cut around the patterns, add at least an extra inch (2.5 cm) on each side. You'll find it a lot easier to have too much rather than too little material to grasp when you pull it into place. And you might discover you've made a mistake somewhere that you can fudge if you have a spare inch or two of fabric to play with. You can always cut excess off when you're finished. If your new fabric is ironable, iron your new pieces before moving to the next step.

7 Tack your new fabric in place. Again, a few suggestions:

■ Tack one side of a section in place (the seat, for example), pull the fabric taut, then attach its opposite side.

■ Once you have two opposite sides attached, pull the fabric taut again, tack the center of the third side, and work outward toward the corners, then do the same for the fourth side. After attaching the first piece of fabric, wait 24 hours or so before continuing, to see how the fabric reacts and how your technique holds up.

■ Things get a little tricky if the furniture has an upholstered back. Start by deciding the placement of the top edge. Tack the top two corners down from underneath, then flip the fabric out of the way. With tacks, apply a strip of cardboard across and flush with the back's top edge, to give it a crisp look when you fold the fabric back over it. For the sides, you can use tack strips (strips of cardboard or metal that have tacks already in them, both available at upholstery supply shops). The metal strips will pull the fabric taut more easily, but don't have as smooth a finished appearance. If you don't want to go to the trouble of hidden edges, you can simply cut your fabric with a ½-inch (1.3 cm) seam allowance, iron it under, and use decorative tacks on the outside to affix the material to the back.

■ Ask a friend to help. Though you can do it alone, four hands are more effective than two when it comes to pulling the fabric evenly taut as you attach it. (The fabric will relax a little, so you do need to make sure it's as tight as possible when you tack it in place.)

■ You may have to make notches on the edges of the fabric to ease it around curves or corners smoothly; refer to the original fabric for clues about where this may be necessary.

■ Don't get worked up if you make mistakes: you'll quickly discover that tacked upholstery is very forgiving. Pull up the tacks, perform a dry run of how you think it works, and try again!

8 Reattach your piece's legs if you removed them.

Tie knots at the four corners. You could also use tassels, rope, or hemp to gather the corners.

problem

Take your pick: ugly table (maybe you're the lucky recipient of your parents' plastic patio furniture), boring table (it'd look better beside the bed in a budget motel), table that's the wrong color or style (if only you had decorated everything else in candy-sweet pastel).

quick fix

Buy a floor-length sarong, or pull one out of the closet that you hardly ever wear. These wraparound skirts that come in everything from solid-colored raw silk to bold tropical prints make versatile tie-on table covers.

Make tight rolls on two sides, and roll the ends into rosettes.

Billow two sides, and tie a knot in the center of each.

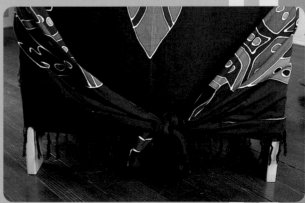

composition in canvas

On the off chance you're not yet in a position to invest in expensive abstract art, here's a pretty darn impressive alternative. The work involved is fittingly minimal; you're simply painting prestretched canvases. The artistic part is choosing your shapes, sizes, colors, and hanging configuration. Toss around terms such as "nonrepresentational" and "reductionist style" as you go, and you'll have no trouble at all.

WHAT YOU NEED

Primed, prestretched canvases (Both art and craft stores sell these in a variety of shapes and sizes. When in doubt, buy the sizes that are on sale.)

Liquid acrylic craft paint in a variety of colors

Paintbrush

Picture-hanging hardware

Hammer

WHAT YOU DO

1 Apply the paint to the canvases, running all your brush strokes in the same direction and applying the paint evenly. Paint the edges as well as the fronts. Don't use too much paint for your first coat. Let the canvases dry overnight.

2 Apply a second coat of paint to all the canvases, again running your brush strokes in the same direction you did for the first coat.

3 Play with layout patterns on the floor (or use the Plotting Where Your Pictures Go technique, page 55). Experiment with large and small gaps between the canvases, cube-style arrangements, long linear configurations, etc.

4 Once you decide how you want your canvases grouped, use the picture-hanging hardware to hang them.

botanicals under glass

Yellowing documents, mass-produced watercolors of sunsets, needlepoints of kittens in baskets—framed versions of all kinds of bad art are going cheap somewhere at a yard sale or secondhand store near you. Forget what's inside; you're after the inexpensive frames. Here's how to use them to create a classy set of pressed ferns floating between panels of glass.

WHAT YOU NEED

Picture frames with glass

1 fern leaf or other flattish plant leaf per frame

Small bottle of black craft paint

Glass cleaner

Sheets of green vellum paper, 8½ x 11 inches (21.6 x 27.9 cm), 1 per frame

Sheets of heavy white paper, 8½ x 5½ inches (21.6 x 14 cm), 1 per frame

Glue stick

Field guide to wild plant identification

Fine-point pen

Glazier clips, 8 per frame (You can buy these little metal fasteners where glass is sold.)

Chrome ball chain, approximately 4 feet (1.2m) per frame

Pliers

Small paintbrush

Screwdriver with flat blade

Staple gun

WHAT YOU DO

1 Use the pliers to remove the glass and backing from the frames. Take the frames to a glass shop, and order an additional piece of glass cut to fit each.

2 Press your ferns or other leaves between the pages of a phone book weighted down with other heavy books. They should be pressed and dried in about five to seven days.

3 Clean the frames, and paint them all black.

4 Clean all your glass.

5 Position each fern or other leaf on a sheet of white paper, and secure it with a bit of glue. Print the Latin name of the fern or leaf across the bottom of the white paper (this is where the field guide comes in handy).

6 Center each white sheet of paper on a sheet of green velum, and secure it with a dot of glue.

7 Center each leaf-and-paper grouping on a pane of glass. Place another piece of glass on top of each, then place each "sandwich" in a frame.

8 Use two glazier's points per corner (one on each side) to secure the glass in the frames. The points push in easily with the flat blade of a screwdriver.

9 Attach the ends of 4 feet (1.2m) of ball chain to the back of each frame with a staple gun.

pillow talk

Scatter them on the floor around a low table; you have dinner seating. Toss a couple of red ones onto your couch; instant seasonal decorating. From dainty throw-pillow size to full-blown floor cushions, pillows are one of the easiest ways to cozy up a room, reinforce a color scheme, carry out a theme, or make a place look lived in. The plain-Jane, discount-store variety of pillow is also the perfect canvas for adding some personal panache.

buying tips

The way a pillow is constructed will dictate which techniques you can easily use to embellish it. If its cover is removable—look for buttons, a zipper, ties, or an overlapped opening on the back—anything is possible (and simpler), from stamping to beading. If the cover is sewn closed, you can still add all kinds of surface decoration. Or, if you're determined and even mildly sewing savvy, you can carefully rip out the stitching on one side of the pillow, remove the cover, decorate it, then stitch it back in place.

simple pillow transformations

WHAT YOU CAN USE

Premade tassels

Buttons

Upholstery trim

Ribbons, rope, twine, etc.

Embroidered or sequined appliqués

Beads

Vintage handkerchiefs

Silk flowers

Fabric paints

Rubber stamps and fabric ink

WHAT YOU CAN DO

Sew one (or more) matching or contrasting tassels to each corner. Or, stitch a passel of tiny tassels all over the pillow.

Stitch big, bold buttons around the front edges of a pillow, or remove and replace your pillow's existing, boring buttons.

Make a bold move, and neatly stitch a length of bright ball fringe or rickrack around the edges of your pillow.

Center an embroidered appliqué or a colorful handkerchief on the pillow, pin it on, and stitch it.

Cut out simple geometric felt shapes if you can't find them precut. Pin them randomly onto the front of the pillow. Use a blanket or running stitch to attach them to the pillow. Contrasting thread is a nice touch.

Stitch on straight lengths of ribbon, yarn, rope, or twine. Tie bows, and stitch their knots in place to secure them.

Sew tiny, glimmering seed beads all over the pillow. This option is primarily recommended for those with plenty of perseverance and time on their hands (or a good long movie ready to pop into the VCR). Still, if it's the glittery look you're after, this is it.

Sew on bunches or rows of silk flowers—they lend themselves to looks ranging from cute to campy.

Remove the pillow cover, slip a folded newspaper inside it to protect the back side, and paint designs on the front with fabric paint. If your cover isn't removable, go ahead and dab designs on it anyway.

Use fabric inks or dye-based inks and rubber stamps to stamp on a design. Alas, this last is recommended only for removable pillow covers, since you need a flat, sturdy surface to effectively stamp on.

Q U I C K F I X

problem

In your mind's eye, your apartment features just a few bold, dramatic decorative flourishes. Unfortunately, the sports trophies and tiny keepsakes you have to work with in real life aren't making the statement you want.

quick fix

Here's an inexpensive and accessible way to create a contemporary, graphic display. Gather a dozen or more simple black-and-white images from any low-cost source—clip them from fashion magazine ads, illustrated calendars, or used books. Trim them all so they measure 8 x 10 inches (20.3 x 25.4 cm), and stick them in matching, unadorned frames. (Watch discount stores for sales, and you'll be able to buy a bunch cheap. You want black-rimmed frames or all-clear frames that close with metal clips.) Fill most of a wall with three or more evenly spaced rows of your framed pictures.

adding casters

To make your furniture go places, simply attach small wheels on swivels that support moveable weight. Casters are categorized according to how heavy a load they can handle (100-pound [45 kg] load-bearing casters, for example). They also come in two primary styles: one with fixture plates that you screw in place and the other with stems you insert in drilled holes. Screw-in-place casters work best on pieces that feature a flat base area, such as a platform or a wastebasket. If you're adding casters to individual furniture legs, stem-type casters provide sturdier support.

furniture on the move

Equip a piece of furniture with wheels, and it not only takes on an air of industrial chic, but it also becomes a more versatile, flexible unit that's happy to change location to meet your changing needs. Baskets and bins that have been outfitted with casters allow you to wheel a supply of books or magazines right up next to your chair and then out of the way when you're finished. Small tables and benches on wheels make it possible to roll televisions and sound systems from spot to spot—or completely out of sight. And low platforms like this one (consider old doors or legless tabletops) can serve as everything from coffee tables to under-bed storage pallets.

reincarnated table

Using little more than sandpaper and fresh paint, we brought this weather-beaten hand-me-down back to life as a sleek worktable. You can use the same resurrection technique on chairs, benches, stools, shelves, you name it.

WHAT YOU NEED

Small table

Wood filler (if necessary)

Primer (Use gesso as your primer; you can find it at art and craft stores. That way, if the paint already on the table is oil paint, you won't have to remove it first.)

Acrylic paint

Water-based polyurethane

Plastic scraper

Sandpaper (fine and medium grit)

Tack cloth

Paintbrush and/or sponge brush (Brushes that are about 1 to 2 inches [2.5 to 5.1 cm] wide work well on smaller furniture pieces.)

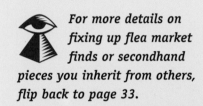

For more details on fixing up flea market finds or secondhand pieces you inherit from others, flip back to page 33.

WHAT YOU DO

1 Don't worry if the table has paint on it from its previous life; there's no need to strip it down to bare wood. Just scrape off any cracked or chipped paint, and fill in any cracks, dents, or holes with wood filler.

2 Sand the table with medium-grit sandpaper first, then use a fine-grit sandpaper to smooth the surface.

3 Wipe down the table with the tack cloth to remove all the sanding dust.

4 Coat the table with primer. Once it's dry, you may need to lightly sand the primer layer with fine-grit sandpaper, so it's smooth. Again, remove all the sanding dust with the tack cloth.

5 Paint the table with the acrylic paint.

6 Let the table dry for at least 24 hours, then coat it with polyurethane. You can apply a second and even third coat of polyurethane if you want the table to be super wear resistant. Wait 24 hours between each coat.

artificial turf trays

If you don't want your guests to take you too seriously, serve them their fruit-punch cocktails atop an artificial garden, aquarium, or night sky under glass. You can use these kitschy compositions as portable trays. Or, mass a collection of them close together on TV-tray stands, and you've got a coffee table that also serves as a conversation piece.

WHAT YOU NEED

Artificial grass in green, blue, and black (Choose the type with the lowest grass height—which is also, oh happy coincidences, the cheapest.)

Plastic trays with lips

⅛-inch (3mm) glass or plastic, cut to fit your tray (You need one piece per tray. Look for glass suppliers in the phone book; they'll sell you the glass or plastic and cut it to size for a small charge.)

Artificial daisies, sheet of orange craft foam and fish stencils, wiggly eyes, silver star garland and gold confetti stars, or any other flat trinkets that suit your fancy

Craft glue

Needle and black thread

Scissors

Craft knife (optional)

Hot glue gun and glue sticks

WHAT YOU DO

daisies on green

1 Use the scissors to cut the green mat to fit the recess in your tray.

2 Pull the daisy heads off their stems, and pull any green plastic off the bases of the flowers, to make them as flat as possible. Trim any amount of stem remaining on the bases of the flowers to about ⅛ inch (3mm).

3 Place the flowers randomly on the mat. Hot glue them in place, if you like.

4 Lay the glass on top of the flower-studded grass.

fish on blue

1 Use the scissors to cut the blue mat to fit the recess in your tray.

2 Trace several fish shapes and sizes onto the foam, and cut them out with scissors or a craft knife. To give them added dimension, hold the knife at a 45° angle while you cut, with the point aiming toward the inside of the fish shape. Flip the angle-cut fish over before you use them.

3 Hot glue wiggly eyes on some of the fish, if you like.

4 Arrange the fish on the mat, and glue them down with hot glue.

5 Lay the glass on top of the fishy mat.

stars on black

1 Use the scissors to cut the black mat to fit the recess in your tray.

2 Arrange the silver star garland on the mat. Use the needle and thread to tack it down every few inches.

3 With craft glue, glue down the garland's stars. You'll probably have to hold them down or put a light weight on top of them until they adhere to the mat. You might also want to pull off extra stars that make the look too busy.

4 Sprinkle gold stars on top of the display.

5 Lay the glass on top of the starry sky.

problem

Cabinets and drawers in your kitchen and bath that feature the same dull, sea-mist gray veneer as the cabinets and drawers in every other cookie-cutter apartment in the city. Or (you decide which is worse), cabinets and drawers that look as if they were salvaged from the kitchen of the camper your parents bought when you were seven.

quick fix

Replacing the handles and knobs of the doors and drawers you open every day can do wonders to liven them up and make them look like your own. Home improvement stores carry a huge variety of both industrial-look and contemporary styles. At smaller home-decor shops, you can find everything from painted-glass knobs to hammered-metal handles. Best of all, you can remove these custom pieces and take them with you when you move on.

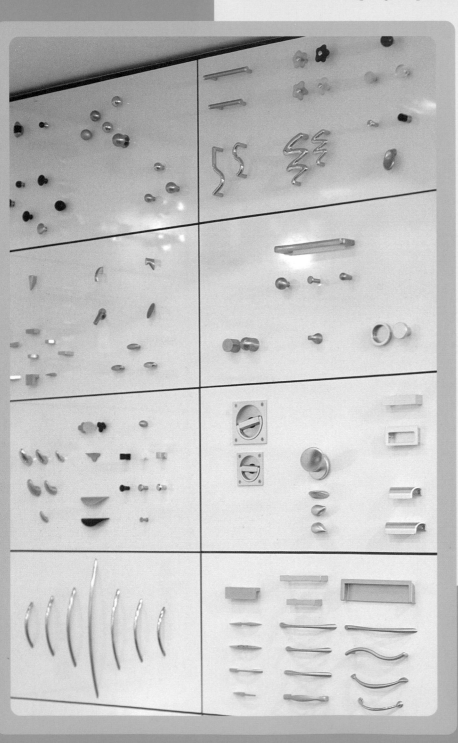

urban jungle

Even if you're cultivating a look that's ultra modern, somewhere amid all the steel pipe, glass block, and shiny metal, you need some living, oxygen-emitting green. Plants are one of the most effective accent pieces you can invest in if you want atmosphere. They can fill bare corners, drape tendrils along bookshelves, climb lattice in windowsills, and cast interesting shadows when lit just right. They look best doing all of this if they're sitting in something other than the plastic containers they're sold in. Here are several suggestions for easy, less-predictable ways to contain plants.

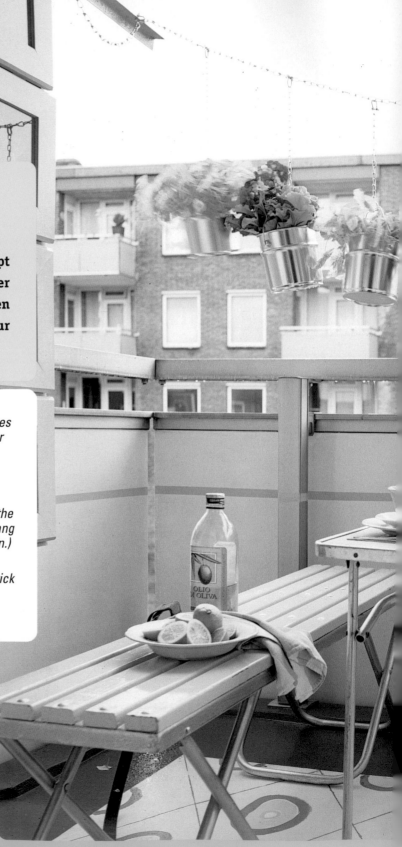

hanging buckets

If you don't have a balcony, adapt this idea—perhaps using smaller buckets—to fit across your kitchen windows or along the wall in your steamy, well-lit bathroom.

WHAT YOU NEED

Galvanized paint pails (Hardware stores are the place for these. For smaller pails, try craft stores.)

S hooks, 2 per pail

2 screw hooks, heavy duty

Length of chain (Buy enough to span the space you want to cover and to hang each bucket from the central chain.)

Drill and drill bits (Use masonry bits if you're hanging your buckets on brick or concrete-block walls.)

Pliers, for tightening S hooks

WHAT YOU DO

1 Before you head out to buy your supplies, measure the width of the space you want to span, and jot down the measurement. Also, decide how many buckets you want to hang in the space and how far you want each to hang from the central chain. When you purchase the chain, the person helping you at the home improvement store will have to cut it from a roll. With your measurements in hand, you can ask the helpful salesperson to make your job easier by cutting one long length for your central chain and multiple short lengths for your hangers.

2 Determine how high you want to mount your long chain. Drill pilot holes in the wall, screw in the screw hooks, and hang the chain from the hooks.

3 Attach a short length of chain to the central chain with an S hook. Hang a bucket on this short length with another S hook. Hang all of your buckets following this same process.

4 If the long chain droops too far, simply adjust the chain at either end until you're satisfied with its amount of sag.

5 You can plant directly into the buckets if you're hanging them outside, just pierce drainage holes in their bases with a hammer and nail first. If you're hanging them inside, put your plants in small plastic containers with drainage holes, then set them down in the buckets.

vintage canisters

Flea markets and yard sales are overflowing with colored-glass containers once used to hold flour and sugar. We turned ours into a windowsill garden that does a spectacular job of catching the afternoon light. Simply wash the canisters well in hot, soapy water, and fill them with potting soil and plants. To add to the sparkly effect of these, we mixed iridescent glass discs (the kind sold to hold flower stems in place) with the soil.

containers within containers

Put your plant in any old nondescript pot. Put a drip tray underneath it, and set it down inside something—almost anything—else. If they don't have to be in direct contact with dirt, roots, and water, all sorts of unusual objects can become holders for plants.

ANTIQUE BIRD CAGES
(Leave the door open, and let the plant weave its way out.)

CERAMIC CHIMNEY FLUES
(Check salvage yards.)

OLD ENAMEL PITCHERS AND WASH BASINS

SHOPPING BAGS LINED WITH BRIGHT TISSUE PAPER
(Imagine a tree-sized plant popping out the top.)

WOODEN CRATES
(Try fruit and vegetable stands as sources.)

LARGE OUTDOOR URNS
(Garden centers sell them. They can fill big, undecorated voids in your apartment with rustic, Tuscan-villa flair.)

A WICKER PICNIC BASKET

AN UPSIDE-DOWN SOMBRERO
(Think cactus.)

BUBBLEWRAP ENVELOPES
(Graphic, urban, high tech.)

apartment-friendly plants

Here are five recommendations—all appropriate for beginning indoor gardeners—for the greening of your apartment.

PHILODENDRONS

Among the easiest houseplants to grow, many philodendrons tolerate low light and lots of neglect. Treat yours well, however, and it'll be beautiful for years.

The name philodendron actually refers to a diverse group of plants whose vines feature heart-shaped leaves ranging from 3 inches (7.6 cm) to 3 feet (.9 m) long. Some types have glossy, solid green leaves, others have velvety leaves with patterns, and still others have deep red leaves and stems. You can limit the size of vining types by keeping their supports small and by training and pruning. The self-heading types eventually can become very large and need ample space. Locate these plants out of heavy traffic paths.

Most philodendrons prefer indirect sunlight and can survive in low light. The common heartleaf philodendron is particularly forgiving of dim environments. Philodendrons like night temperatures of 65 to 70°F (18.3 to 21°C) and day temperatures of 75 to 85°F (23.9 to 29.4°C). Water them frequently enough to keep the soil evenly moist, but not soggy. Never let your plant stand in water. High humidity is ideal for best growth, but philodendrons will put up with the low level of humidity in most homes. Fertilize philodendrons regularly with a dilute water-soluble houseplant fertilizer, following the manufacturer's recommendations, or use a time-release fertilizer.

SPIDER PLANTS

There's one main reason spider plants are one of the most common houseplants: instant gratification. Spider plants grow quickly and easily to 2 to 2½ feet (61 to 76.2 cm) wide and 2 to 3 feet (61 to 91.4 cm) long when grown in hanging baskets, and they're especially speedy when it comes to forming new plant shoots. Their long, grassy leaves can be green or striped yellow or white. Long wiry stems appear on healthy plants, with many small white flowers and miniature plantlets sprouting off their tips. These new plantlets will root if they touch soil. Detach them to produce new plants, or leave them on to create a very full basket.

Spider plants grow best in bright, indirect light. They can tolerate some direct sunlight, but midday light may scorch their leaves. They prefer temperatures between 65 and 75°F (18.3 and 23.9°C) during the day, and 50 to 55°F (10 to 12.8°C) at night. During the winter, move spider plants a few feet from windows to protect them from drafts. These plants should dry out briefly between watering. During times of active growth, feed them a water-soluble or a time-release houseplant fertilizer, following the label recommendations.

RUBBER PLANTS

Excellent plants for beginners, rubber plants grow well in a variety of conditions. Their glossy, leathery leaves vary in color from dark green to deep maroon, and sometimes have yellow, cream, pink, or white markings. The trees easily reach 6 to 10 feet (1.8 to 3 meters) or more indoors if they have enough space; support them with a stake. You can prune them to reduce their size or to rejuvenate them (which may be necessary in the spring).

Rubber plants prefer bright light, but will adapt to low light. They grow best with the morning light from an east window. Their ideal temperature ranges from 60 to 65°F (15.5 to 18.3°C) at night and 75 to 80°F (23.9 to 26.7°C) during the day. Water rubber plants thoroughly, letting the soil dry somewhat between watering. They prefer humid conditions, but tolerate the dry air common in homes. Wash the leaves with water when they get dusty to keep them looking healthy. Fertilize your rubber plant regularly with a water-soluble houseplant fertilizer during active growth, following the manufacturer's recommendations. Fertilize plants growing in lower light less often.

WHEAT GRASS AND SPROUTS

Growing grassy plants inside in everything from collections of ceramic bowls to long metal troughs is an especially contemporary way to add living green to your indoor environment. It's also a great reminder of one of the benefits of apartment dwelling: no mowing.

Soak wheat berries (you can purchase these at health food stores) overnight at room temperature. The seeds will double in size. Fill the container you want to plant them in with 2 inches (5.1 cm) of soil, and water it well. Cover the soil completely with seeds, so you can't see it, then cover the seeds with a light sprinkling of soil. Mist the top layer of soil with a water bottle, and put the container in filtered sunlight (in front of closed blinds, for example). Mist the soil daily, but don't soak it. The seeds should sprout within four days; place them in sunlight and keep misting. They should reach a height of 6 inches (15.2 cm) within a week to 10 days. For different plant textures, you can also sprout alfalfa seeds or lentils.

FERNS

Ferns with tough, leathery foliage usually adapt better to typical household conditions than feathery, delicate types. Most ferns prefer moderate, indirect light inside; direct sunlight will damage the foliage. Close to a north-facing window is an ideal spot for a fern. Never put one directly in a south or west-facing window. Because fern fronds are sensitive to rough handling, you should also keep ferns out of high-traffic areas where they might be brushed up against regularly.

The ideal temperature range for most ferns is between 60 and 70°F (15.5 and 21°C) during the day, and about 50 to 60°F (10 to 15.5°C) at night. All ferns love moisture, but the amount they need varies among the many different types. Some like being kept almost wet, while others should dry slightly between waterings. Don't allow any fern to dry out completely, though. Likewise, don't allow water to stand in pots; it can lead to root damage. Also, lightly mist your fern occasionally to replicate its natural environment. Homes usually have too low a humidity for fine, thin-leafed ferns, and in the winter, the humidity level drops even lower—a good time to move your fern to your most humid room: the bathroom. Fertilize most ferns lightly once a month, from April through September only. Apply liquid houseplant fertilizers at about half the recommended rate. Their leaves will scorch if they're fertilized too heavily.

wild side table

When all your carefully selected neutral colors and go-with-anything styles start to make you feel you're living in an environment that's a tad too tame, follow these four easy steps. They tell you how to turn an ordinary-looking end table or other piece of paintable furniture into something much less civilized.

WHAT YOU NEED

Table

Photo or drawing of animal stripes or spots you want to copy

Pencil

Acrylic primer

Acrylic paints (You need one light color such as white or cream and one dark color such as black or brown. If you're tackling a design with more than two colors—maybe leopard spots—you'll also need some in-between shades such as caramel or dark gold.)

Paintbrushes

Sandpaper

Tack cloth

WHAT YOU DO

1 If your table is made of raw, unpainted wood, you'll want to give it a coat or two of acrylic primer. If it's already been painted or varnished, sand it to give it "tooth" to accept new coats of paint, wipe up the sanding residue with the tack cloth, then add a coat of acrylic primer.

2 Give the table a base coat of your lighter paint, and let it dry. Give the table a second coat of paint. Let the second coat dry as well.

3 Study the design you want to copy. You'll see that it's composed of broad areas of one color and accented with other colors. A zebra design is the simplest in terms of color: you'll use black and white. A tiger or ocelot design may use three or more colors. Lightly sketch the large stripes or spots of your design onto the table. Don't be too precise. Concentrate your design on the top of the table, then extend it to the legs, wrapping the design around each leg.

4 Outline the stripes or spots with a small brush and your darker color of paint, then fill them in. Stand back, squint your eyes, and see if you think you need to add smaller, thinner stripes or spots in places. Just take it gradually; it's easier to add accents than it is to remove them. Let the paint dry. Give the stripes or spots additional coats of paint, if necessary.

flea-market shopping

With their one-of-a-kind finds and bargain prices, flea markets are a great place for taking some decorating risks on fabric, furniture, and accents. Here are tips for making the most of a flea-market trip.

● Dedicated flea market shoppers are up at the crack of dawn. Arrive early so you're there for the best selection.

● Take a list of your needs for each room. Do let the spontaneous spirit of flea-market shopping guide you, but don't stray too far from your list. (A collection of Neil Diamond eight-tracks might make an interesting living room centerpiece, but it doesn't satisfy your need for a coffee table.)

● Take a set of room photos, paint chips, or fabric swatches if you're trying to match colors.

● If you're shopping for furniture, be sure to drive to the flea market in a vehicle equipped to transport your purchases home with you.

● Take cash in small bills. Some sellers can make change or will take checks; others can't or won't.

● Negotiating prices is usually acceptable, so use this as an excuse to sharpen your bargaining skills.

● Sometimes, the only way to know if the pink chenille bedspread or the mirror whose frame could use some polishing is right is to take it home, clean it up, and give it a try. Give yourself a "why not?" budget for seductive finds that you just aren't sure about.

● Beware of furniture made with veneer (a thin layer of wood applied atop the basic structure) or particle board (chips of wood glued together). You generally can't refurbish either.

nesting tables makeover

You've seen them. Every mega-discount store with a furniture aisle sells them—styleless table sets with a shiny finish that look as if they should be displaying business cards and brochures in some office lobby. Upside: they're affordable and handy. Downside: woefully ordinary. Here's a smashing way to overcome that little problem with a bit of paint and decoupage gloss and an extra-large photocopy of a face.

WHAT YOU NEED

*Black-and-white photo of your
face or another you won't
mind looking at regularly*

Set of nesting tables

Water-based primer/sealer

*Acrylic latex enamel in gloss
white, gloss red, and gloss
black*

Decoupage gloss medium

Acrylic paint in silver and gold

*Clear acrylic enamel spray
(glossy)*

Sandpaper, fine

Tack cloth

*Paintbrush, 1 to 1½ inch
(2.5 to 3.8 cm)*

Ruler

Craft knife or scissors

*Plastic lid or something similar
to use as a paint palette*

Small, round artist's brush

Rectangular kitchen sponge

WHAT YOU DO

1 Create two large copies of your photo. Enlarge the photo first on a standard photocopy machine, then make two larger copies of the enlarged image on a poster-size copy machine (you can find them at commercial copy shops).

2 Sand your tables thoroughly, to cut through whatever finish is already on the wood (it'll keep your paint from adhering well). Use the tack cloth to wipe the sanding dust off the tables.

3 Apply primer/sealer to all parts of the tables with the paintbrush. Let it dry. If much of the table is showing through, apply a second coat to the table you'll be painting white. Clean the paintbrush.

4 Paint your tables: one white, one black, and one red. Start with the tables upside down, and paint the undersides of the tops, the aprons, and the legs. When the tables are dry enough to flip over, do so and paint the tops. You don't need to paint the areas where you'll apply the images. Simply paint a border of approximately ⅛ inch (3 mm) on the top surfaces. Clean your brush between colors and when you finish.

5 Measure the area you want to cover on each tabletop. Using the measurements, mark out the areas you want to cut from the photocopies. You'll cut the eye area from one photocopy, the mouth area from the other photocopy, and the nose area from the first photocopy. (The parts you want to cut of the nose and mouth area will likely overlap; that's why you need the two photocopies.) Cut out the face pieces.

6 Apply the decoupage gloss to the tabletop areas you'll be covering, using the paintbrush and following the instructions on the bottle. Place your images, smooth out any air bubbles, and let everything dry.

7 Brush decoupage gloss over the images and onto the painted border, to seal the edges. Let everything dry.

8 Pour a bit of gold paint into the plastic lid. Load one end of the rectangular sponge with paint, and sponge it lightly on the aprons of the tables. The right angle on the edge of the rectangle shape should fit the apron perfectly, creating clean sponged edges. Let the paint dry.

9 Decide where you want to add star and dot accents on the decoupaged images. Pour some silver paint in your plastic lid, and paint them on with the small artist's brush. Use the end of the brush dipped in paint to create the dots (moving it straight up and down). You can either paint the stars freehand or cut out a star image and lightly trace it onto the tables first.

10 Spray the tables all over (tops, aprons, and legs) with clear acrylic spray. It'll help with durability and take away the tacky feel of the dried decoupage gloss.

storage

Never mind *how* someone with zero discretionary income can accumulate so much stuff. You can. You likely already have. And without some clever storage solutions, it'll clutter up every spec of your cozy little living space.

shelving five ways

Sure, your apartment may have a lot of what a professional organizer would call "underutilized storage space." Trouble is, it comes in the form of a long, skinny strip of wall above the bedroom door or a narrow nook between the stove and fridge, and you can't find shelves to fit. Good news from the do-it-yourself front: if you can nail four pieces of wood together, you can make your own shelves to fit wherever you want them.

WHAT YOU DO

1 Smooth the edges of the brackets and the front and side edges of the shelf with sandpaper. Leave the back edge of the shelf and the top edges of the shelf back unsanded; they need to be square so they'll fit together accurately. Finish sand both sides of the brackets, the top of the shelf, and the front of the shelf back.

2 Fasten the brackets to the ends of the shelf back by applying a small amount of wood glue first, then using three or four nails on each end. Be sure to align the top and rear edges of each bracket with the top and rear of the shelf back.

3 Fasten the shelf to the back and brackets, again using glue first, then nailing.

If you're a perfectionist, buy or borrow a tool called a nail set, which you can use to drive the nails below the wood's surface. You can then fill the nail holes with wood filler, so all the edges are smooth.

WHAT YOU NEED

2 pieces of wood, one to be the shelf top and one that's a bit shorter in length to be the back (Paint-grade lumber and medium-density fiberboard are both fine choices for shelves you plan to paint or finish in some way. You can either buy your wood cut to size or cut it yourself with a handsaw.)

2 wooden brackets (Home improvement stores sell manufactured wooden brackets in a range of styles.)

Sandpaper

8d finish nails

Wood glue

Hammer

four easy variations on the theme

VARIATION 1:
ADDING A TOWEL BAR

Before assembling the shelf, drill two ¾-inch (1.9 cm) holes ⅜ inch (9.5 mm) deep in the two end brackets. Position the holes 2 inches (5.1 cm) from the back edge of the brackets and 1½ inches (3.8 cm) from the bottom, and be sure you drill in opposite sides of each bracket, creating mirror-image pieces. Insert a ¾-inch (1.9 cm) hardwood dowel into the holes, then assemble the shelf.

VARIATION 2:
ADDING A LOWER SHELF

Cut a board to size. Sand the top, the bottom, and the front edge, but leave both ends and the back edges square. Decide where you want it to attach to the brackets. Using a square, lightly draw a line at that point on each bracket, making the line perpendicular to the rear edge of the bracket. You'll use the lines to align the bottom edge of the shelf with the brackets while nailing. Use a couple of nails in each end and across the back to fasten the lower shelf in place.

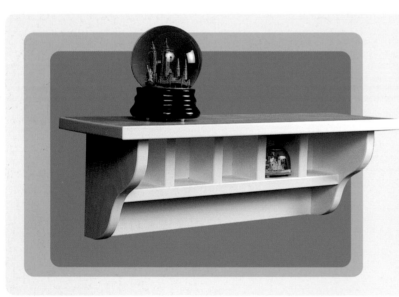

VARIATION 3:
ADDING PIGEONHOLES

Add the lower shelf in Variation 2, then measure the opening between your lower shelf and the top one to determine the height of your pigeonhole dividers. The length of the dividers should match the depth of the lower shelf. Cut the number of dividers you want. Using a square, mark guidelines where each divider will go, making the lines perpendicular to the front edge of the lower shelf. Sand the dividers, position them, then drive a couple of nails through the top and bottom shelves to fasten them in place.

VARIATION 4:
ADDING PEGS

Figure the number of pegs you want, purchase them, then make evenly spaced marks for each on your shelf back, about 1 inch (2.5 cm) up from the bottom edge. Drill holes the size of the ends of your pegs at each mark. Add a small amount of wood glue to the holes, then insert the pegs.

hanging shelves

How you secure a shelf to a wall depends on what type of wall you've got.

- If you're working with a hollow, wood-frame wall, the easiest approach is to drive support screws through the shelf and the plaster or drywall and into a piece of that wooden framing. Make sure that at least half the screw's length extends into the framing piece. If you're mounting your shelf to a hollow part of the wall (where there's no framing member to screw into), you need to first drill holes in the wall and insert anchors (see the next point). They'll help hold your screws or bolts in place.

- If you're working on solid masonry walls, the screws or bolts you use to hang your shelves need to work in conjunction with some sort of anchor that expands and grips inside the wall. Lead anchors and expansion shields are both standard choices. Hardware stores sell them.

A basic home improvement book will provide you with an illustrated chart of wall fasteners and tell you what sort of wall and shelf weight each is best suited for. The folks at your local hardware store can also help guide you toward the right fastener for the job.

energy savers

There are plenty of ways to lower your energy bills without cramping your style. Here are both year-round and seasonal habits you can cash in on.

YEAR-ROUND:

- Turn off all lights, stereos, and other electrical equipment when you're not using them.

- Turn the heat down or the air conditioning up a few degrees while you sleep and before you leave home for the day.

- If you have access to your hot water heater, keep the temperature at 110°F (43°C). You'll still enjoy steamy showers, but you'll have a lower energy bill.

- Install aerators in all your faucets and a low-flow showerhead to reduce the amount of water you use. (These are inexpensive and easy to install. Just be sure to choose a good brand that guarantees decent water pressure. If it doesn't deliver, return it.)

WINTER:

- If you've got a window-unit air conditioner, wrap it in plastic and seal the edges with duct tape. This will keep warm air from leaking out around it.

- Weatherstrip your windows. Weatherstripping is a modern plastic creation available at all hardware stores. It seals the cracks around windows where air can sneak in or out. Make sure the surfaces where you want to apply it are clean and dry and that it's at least 20°F (-7°C) out, then follow the directions on the product's box.

- If your apartment is especially drafty, seal entire windows with clear plastic sold at hardware stores and home centers for this purpose. First, clean and dry the molding around your window. Next, apply a line of double-sided tape along the entire window frame. Press the plastic wrap firmly to the tape, covering the entire window. The plastic will wrinkle; don't worry about it. Finally, use a hair dryer on its highest setting and blow hot air evenly over the entire covering. The hot air will shrink the plastic wrap, sealing your window completely. At the end of the season, remove the plastic and the tape.

the indispensable
(and amazingly easy to build) cube

Build one. Admit how easy it was—and how great it looks. Build a bunch more, and paint them all different colors. Hang your cubes and organize your heart out.

WHAT YOU NEED

2 pieces of ½-inch-thick (1.3cm) wood for the cube's sides

2 pieces of ½-inch-thick (1.3cm) wood for the cube's top and bottom (These pieces need to be 1 inch [2.5cm] longer than the two side pieces.)

1 piece of ¼-inch (6mm) plywood for the back (This piece should be a square, with its sides the same length as your top and bottom pieces.)

Wood glue

Hammer

8d finish nails

⅝-inch (1.6cm) wire nails or brads

Sandpaper

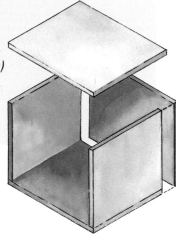

WHAT YOU DO

1 Brush wood glue onto the edges of your pieces, then nail the top and bottom to the sides.

2 Check to make sure your cube is square, then apply a small amount of glue to the edges of the back piece and nail it in place, using ⅝-inch (1.6cm) wire nails or brads.

3 Smooth all the edges of the cube with sandpaper.

problem

You don't consider it a problem, exactly. You like to think of it as being well pre-pared: a different pair of sunglasses for every mood, bracelets to match any out-fit, enough beer mugs to host the whole volleyball team. Nevertheless, coming up with places to put all these reserve supplies is somewhat of a dilemma.

quick fix

Fortunately, one person's storage problem is another's decorating device. If your items can be loosely grouped into something resembling a collection—hats, scarves, flower vases, you get the idea—pull them out of your overflowing closet or cabi-net, and put them front and center. That can mean everything from hanging them on hooks you mount in the hallway to lining them up on a sunny windowsill.

making the one-room efficiency work

"Studio living" seems chic when you read about it in magazine spreads accompanied by glossy photos of airy, high-ceilinged, chrome-and-white interiors. But in real life, the experience can be just plain crowded. Here are some tips and simple decorating tricks for helping a one-room apartment both look and feel more livable.

PAINT. A neutral tone will help your place seem as expansive as possible. Still desperate for color? Paint one wall to contrast with the off-white or cream of the others. Just avoid dark colors; they tend to swallow space.

LAYOUT. Dividing your apartment into sections can create the illusion of a much larger space. Strategic placement of a couch can say: "This is the living area, back there is the bedroom." A standing divider or a few tall plants can screen off where you sleep from where you eat and entertain. The trick is not to go overboard. Too many dividing devices, and you'll feel as if you live in a maze.

ORGANIZATION. Clutter is your enemy. Avoid knickknacks, letting just a few bold pieces of artwork or decoration add flavor, color, and pizazz instead. Mount shelves on the wall to free floor space. Select kitchen appliances that fit under cabinets, so they're not filling up your small amount of counter space. Invest heavily in hooks, hangers, knobs, and specialty storage pieces designed to keep the tools of daily life in their place and, when possible, out of full view.

STORAGE. Use your interior cabinet space to the max. Hooks or magnetic strips will make it possible for you to hang mugs and utensils inside the doors, freeing shelves for other items. If you don't have lots of cabinet and closet space, minimize your supplies and possessions to what you absolutely need. Put what you have to on "display" (think flea-market dishes, canned and boxed foods with pretty labels, decorative boxes holding winter sweaters, etc.).

FURNITURE. Select furniture that does double duty. Chairs with removable seats can conceal extra sheets and blankets. Stools and ottomans with detachable lids are excellent hiding places for office supplies, books, and odds and ends. A futon that folds up into a couch and down into a bed is a great idea for a small room. Keep a table uncluttered so it can be used as a food preparation area, an ironing board, and a craft area. Cover it with a bright tablecloth that matches your decor.

ILLUSIONS. Create space out of thin air. If your one-room palace didn't come with a closet, several extra-long pegs can double as coat hooks and a closet area. (You can even fit a stack of several skirts or pairs of jeans on top of side-by-side pegs.) Drape a tapestry or pretty piece of fabric to protect your clothes from dust and mimic a closet door. For a room without a view, paint a window on a wall. (You can even adjust the view to suit the season.) Faking a doorway is just as easy. Both options are surprisingly effective at relieving that cramped feeling. They also show what a good—and good-humored—sport you are.

storage in disguise

In the space-deprived reality of first apartments, few storage containers are as handy as those that masquerade—and do double duty—as something else. Create a coffee table out of a wooden trunk, for example, and you've got a flat surface for drinks, candles, or plates of food on top, but also a nice hollow space hidden below for stashing winter blankets, yearbooks, or a few pieces of camping gear. What makes this arrangement so apartment friendly, of course, is that the multitasking trunk does all of this without demanding a single inch more of your precious floor space than most standard coffee tables would.

Here's a starter list of other unconventional storage containers that can successfully pose as everything from coffee tables and nightstands to end tables and bases for televisions and sound-systems:

- *Metal file bins*
- *Lidded wicker baskets*
- *Wooden wine cases*
- *Barrels*
- *Wall-mount kitchen cabinets (unmounted, of course)*
- *Stacked sets of secondhand suitcases*
- *Large aluminum tool chests (the kind designed to fit in the back of pickup trucks)*
- *Displaced wooden drawers fitted into plywood boxes*

lattice organizer

Got a tall, skinny stretch of wall or a long, narrow strip that you know would be the perfect place for hanging pots and pans or back scrubbers and towels? This eclectically studded strip of lattice is the way to make use of it. The bare lattice comes ready-made at home improvement stores, and it's easy to saw to size yourself. Then you screw all your showy hangers into it, rather than into the wall. Landlord is happy. You're happy. And everything has a place to hang.

WHAT YOU NEED

Ready-made lattice
   (Buy a strip that's close to the size you need; you can trim it when you get it home.)

Pickling stain

Liquid dye in any color you like

Variety of hangers
   (Here's your chance to show off a few funky [and pricier] drawer and cabinet pulls or knobs, plus hooks, handles, pulleys, etc. You don't need a whole expensive set of anything, just one of each.)

Handsaw

Paintbrush

Rags

Screwdriver

Drill and small drill bits (optional)

WHAT YOU DO

1 With the handsaw, cut your lattice to fit the nook or cranny in which you want to position it.

2 Paint the front and all the edges of the lattice with the pickling stain. As you work, wipe off excess pickling stain with a rag every three to five minutes. Let the stain dry while you clean your brush.

3 Paint the dye over the pickling stain, wiping it randomly in various places, so more of the white pickling stain shows through here and there. This gives your organizer a washed-out, weathered look. Let the paint dry.

4 Screw your hangers where you want them on the lattice. To make this easier, you can first drill pilot holes one size smaller than the screws you're using.

 Don't screw or drill too closely to the lattice's edges or the wood will split.

problem

All those handy storage spots (the attic, the garage, the walk-in closet) are way back at your parents' house—not here where you need them.

quick fix

If you're honest, you'll probably admit that this is not the first time it's occurred to you that the wide-open space beneath a bed is just the spot for shoving all kinds of items you don't plan to use within the next five minutes. Into that concealed expanse where perhaps you once nudged crumb-covered plates or loose articles of clothing, you can now slide metal boxes, rattan baskets, and rolling platforms made to store your more grown-up and neatly organized possessions.

QUICK FIX

coffeehouse magazine racks

Whether you keep up with vegetarian cooking, snowboarding, international politics, or the local arts scene, chances are you have at least one or two magazines appearing in your mailbox every month. Then there are the extras you grab at the newsstand, the alternative weekly you pick up for the movie reviews and horoscopes, and the catalogs full of the supplies you need for the cooking, snowboarding, or whatever.

If, like the owners of well-kept coffeehouses, you don't want all this glossy paper and newsprint cluttering your tables, couches, and floor, follow their lead and install a few wall-mount hanging racks. Home improvement stores carry a huge selection of towel racks, in styles ranging from rustic to high tech. Simply use the screws that come with them to attach them to a wall, and you have a place to keep all that must-have reading material for the 23 hours a day you're not curling up with it.

when all else fails, shop

With companies out there devoted solely to creating custom-shaped gizmos for storing everything from spoons to shoes, it's likely that one or two of the items they've come up with are just what you need to put your place in order. You'll find storage solutions for sale in three basic categories.

freestanding storage

The main advantage of freestanding storage is that it's portable and therefore adaptable. Bookcases, carts, metal shelving units, and furniture pieces such as tables equipped with drawers or doors all fall into this category. For even more flexibility, opt for freestanding storage pieces that feature adjustable components (such as shelves you can move to meet your needs) and that are outfitted with wheels, so that rolling the piece here and there (and out of the way) is a no-fuss job.

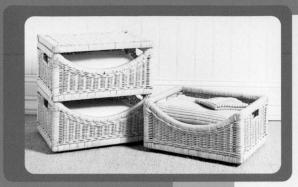

compartmentalized storage

Many times, simply keeping items separated is the key to storing them neatly and efficiently. A drawer divided into distinct sections of rubber bands, paper clips, thumbtacks, and staples, for example, is easier to navigate than one full of a nondescript mass of home-office supplies. Anything that helps segregate pieces into those helpful, partitioned sections can be thought of as compartmentalized storage, from baskets, jars, and bags to hooks and pegs.

item-specific storage

These storage pieces are specially designed to perform specific functions, such as organize your CD collection, keep all the shampoo and soap in one place in the shower, or store your cooking supplies and gadgetry close at hand but not all over your one tiny patch of counter space. Sometimes, an item-specific storage piece is all you need to quickly solve a straightforward storage problem.

buyer beware

When you're confronted with all the alluring options, from crates, baskets, trunks, and boxs to bags, racks, and bins, it's tempting to load up on snazzy-looking containers that end up creating even more clutter in your small space—without meeting your actual storage needs. The best defense against this is to have a clear idea of those needs before you hit the store aisles or dial up the catalog company. Buy a box for storing sweaters if that's what you need, not the electric-green canister set that you love but you're not sure what to do with. Also, don't waste precious space housing oversized storage containers. Match the size of your container to the thing to be contained.

pattern for
Painted
File Cabinet

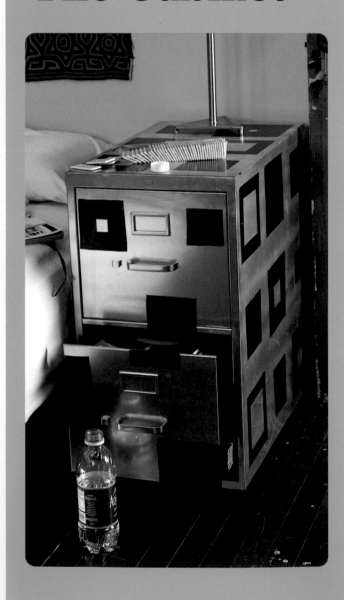

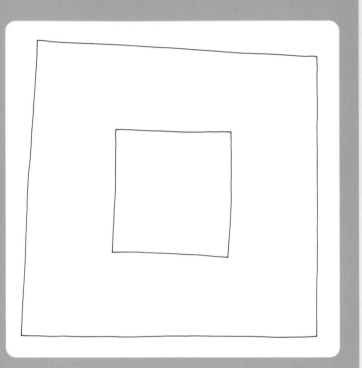

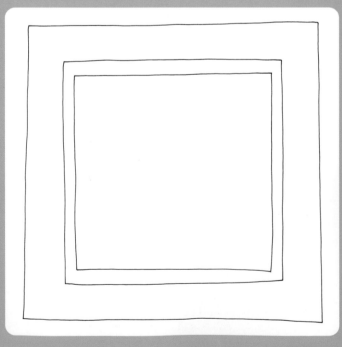

enlarge 200%

acknowledgments

An especially tasteful group of apartment dwellers helped us develop some of our early ideas for this book. Thanks to them all: Cindy Burda, Dietra Garden, Veronika Alice Gunter, Emma Jones, Michelle Keenan, Shelly Mehlen, Charlie Pierce, and Heather Smith.

And while we're at it, extra amounts of very special thanks must be heaped upon Veronika Alice Gunter, research maven, gifted writer, in-house hipster, and, helpfully, a landlord who has rented her share of apartments. She made all the nifty sidebars throughout the book happen.

a note about suppliers

Usually, the supplies you need for making the projects in Lark books can be found at your local craft supply store, discount mart, home improvement center, or retail shop relevant to the topic of the book. Occasionally, however, you may need to buy materials or tools from specialty suppliers. In order to provide you with the most up-to-date information, we have created suppliers listings on our Web site, which we update on a regular basis. Visit us at www.larkbooks.com, click on "Craft Supply Sources," and then click on the relevant topic. You will find numerous companies listed with their web address and/or mailing address and phone number.

contributors

If there's something these amazingly talented people can't whip up with paintbrushes, needles, hammers, glue, and a very strict budget, we'd like to know what it is.

SHEILA ENNIS is a writer and artist living in Boston, Massachusetts. She teaches writing at a local community college and has a small business as a decorative paint finisher. She applies her enthusiasm for crafts to anything that involves paint. Sheila's work appears on page 101.

DIETRA GARDEN lives in Asheville, North Carolina, where she teaches visual arts to elementary-age students. She has worked in the art field as a professional since 1990, teaching in public schools and summer camps, and offering private studio lessons. She also does commissioned work and has recently had her art featured in Art-O-Mat vending machines. Dietra's work appears on pages 59, 70, 73, 74, 90, 135, and 150. She'd like to give special credit and thanks to artist Anna Morgan, who created the batik print in the project on page 70.

DIANA LIGHT lives and works in the beautiful Blue Ridge Mountains of North Carolina. Her home/studio, like her life, is surrounded by glittering glass in hundreds of forms, styles, and types. After earning her B.F.A. in painting and print-making, she extended her expertise to etching and painting fine glass objects. She has contributed to numerous Lark books and is the coauthor of Lark's *The Weekend Crafter: Etching Glass*. Her work appears on pages 122–23, 128, and 140.

SHELLEY LOWELL, of Columbia, Maryland, is an award-winning graphic designer, illustrator, and fine artist. Her paintings and sculpture have been exhibited in museums and galleries in many cities throughout the United States. She has contributed to Lark books ranging from The *Ultimate Clock Book* and *Painting on Glass* to *Creative Candleholders*. Shelley consulted on the projects on pages 78 and 126.

NATHALIE MORNU studied fine craft for five years before pursuing a writing career. The chair on page 113 was her first foray into affixing fabric to furniture. The rest of Nathalie's work appears on pages 92, 98, 110, and 118.

ALLISON SMITH lives in Asheville, North Carolina. Her home-based business specializes in providing deluxe tourist accommodations in remote locations around the world. She is an avid crafter and designer in addition to being a full-time mother. She has created projects for numerous Lark books including *Decorating Baskets*, *Girls' World*, and *Decorating Candles*. Her work appears on pages 68, 117, 120, 131, and 134.

TERRY TAYLOR lives and works in Asheville, North Carolina, as an editor and project coordinator for Lark Books. He is a prolific designer and exhibiting artist, and works in media ranging from metals and jewelry to paper crafts and mosaics. Some of the most recent Lark books to which he has contributed include *Creative Outdoor Lighting*, *Salvage Style*, and *The Book of Wizard Craft*. Terry consulted on the projects on pages 54, 62, 65, 85, 88, 95, 97, 122–23, and 138.

SKIP WADE makes a living making people and places look good. Specializing in fashion and domestics, he works in both still photography and film as a photo stylist, prop master, wardrobe manager, and location scout. He and his partner live in Asheville, North Carolina, where they're continually renovating a 1920's house. He has contributed his talents to several Lark books, including *The New Book of Table Settings*, *Decorating Porches and Decks*, and *Decorating with Mini-Lights*. His own designs appear on pages 82, 87, 94, 100, 106, 107, 124, and 153, and he contributed his styling talents to projects throughout the book.